MACHINE EMBROIDERY
Stitched Patterns
VALERIE CAMPBELL-HARDING

B T BATSFORD

Acknowledgements

Very many thanks to the sewing machine companies who lent me machines so that I could learn the capabilities of all the advanced machines on the market: Chris Thompson at Bernina, my local dealer for the Husqvarna, John Dewing at Janome, and Tina Cowpertwaite at Pfaff and Singer. I would also like to thank my own sewing machine retailer and engineer, Steve Beevis at Salisbury Sewing Machines, for his interest and generosity.

Many thanks to Maggie Grey who is equally interested in computerised sewing machines and came up with some really good ideas and wonderful samples. I am also grateful to my students who often jolted my thinking in another direction.

Jon Walley is a continual help when things go awry with my Macintosh computer and always shows an interest in how we are using computers and computerised sewing machines in our field (most of the diagrams were done in a draw programme called Canvas and some in a paint programme called SuperPaint). The quote on page 7 is from *Creative Machine Embroidery* by Kristen Dibbs, published by Simon & Schuster, Australia.

First published 1997
Reprinted 2000
The paperback editon published 2004

Text, designs and line illustrations © copyright Valerie Campbell-Harding
Photographs © copyright BT Batsford Ltd

The right of Valerie Campbell-Harding to be identified as Author of this work has been asserted by him in accordance with the Copyright, Designs and Patents Act 1988.

ISBN 0 7134 8908 1

A CIP catalogue record for this book is available from the British Library.

Printed in Singapore by Kyodo Printing Co Pte Ltd

for the publishers

B T Batsford
Chrysalis Books Group
The Chrysalis Building
Bramley Road
London W10 6SP

www.batsford.com

An imprint of **Chrysalis** Books Group plc

Contents

INTRODUCTION

Until recently all of us with a passion for machine embroidery were quite content with our reliable, mechanical sewing machines. However as they got older, and we heard our friends raving about their new electronic and computerised machines, the itch to buy a new one became unbearable. In the early days of these new machines there were a number of technical problems, but they have now been redesigned and improved so that they are completely reliable. I find the technology offered by these new models irresistible.

The embroidery and quilting market is now flooded with machines which can decorate fabrics with almost any type of pattern, and more come out every year. Many people are bewildered by the numerous possibilities and the wide range of practical and decorative stitches that even the simplest electronic machines have, let alone those with more complex patterns and larger motifs. However these machines are extremely user-friendly, and absolutely refuse to let you do the wrong thing (such as trying to stitch with the needle lever left up, or with the feed dog dropped when you don't mean to). In addition these advanced machines can stitch at very low speeds with full power, have an automatic needle stop up or down, and a low bobbin warning. Some machines are capable of moving the fabric from side-to-side or diagonally, and can therefore stitch much larger patterns, or stitch in different directions without turning the fabric – a boon when you come to a corner. Once you have used these facilities, you will not want to do without them.

Most machines have similar practical stitches, and cover a selection of the many decorative patterns. They often have the same capabilities and only differ in how they are used – which knob to turn, button to push, or whether you need to press a touch screen or manoeuvre a trackball. Some companies make more stitches and patterns available with memory cards or cassettes which can be stored in the machine's memory and some allow you to design your own. Computer sewing machines can flip the patterns vertically or horizontally and can store changes or combinations of patterns. These machines do have some limitations, as they do not have the specialism of industrial embroidery machines, so you will have to work within the restrictions of your own machine.

Some sewing machines have connecting cables to a computer so that patterns can be downloaded to the machine, or stored on cards. This software is still too limiting to interest me much, and so I have restricted this book to the use of built-in patterns, commercial patterns on memory cards, and the use of separate scanners, as this is such a quick and easy method of stitching your own designs (see Chapter 6).

I have seven sewing machines in my workroom. The Bernina 1630s and the Pfaff 7550 are my own, along with a Bernette overlocker and a Bernette Deco, a dedicated embroidery machine with a scanner. Three are lent to me – a Janome 900 with two scanners, a Pfaff 7570 with an embroidery unit, and a Husquvarna Orchidea. This is definitely overkill – it is not essential to have all these! However using all these machines, combined with others I have used in the past, has given me some insight into the different approaches used by the main manufacturers. I tend to use each machine for a different purpose, and I would get frustrated with only one – I prefer the patterns on one of them, one is better for free machining, one has the reverse button directly over the needle and a marvellous needle threader, one is no good with two threads through the needle but is excellent for the larger motifs – and so on. However, modern sewing machines are so complex that I do recommend using one machine and getting to know it really well. The more you use it, the more you will find it can do for you.

I teach machine embroidery and many of my students have simple swing needle machines with very few stitches, so a good part of this book includes using the simple, practical and decorative patterns common to most machines. The final part of the book focuses on techniques using the more sophisticated machines.

The stitches and patterns on sewing machines are so often unexplored and just used in straight lines to decorate hems, cuffs and the edges of collars, or as a band on bathroom towels. This book is designed for anyone who wishes to do rather more than that and I hope that the many ideas and techniques included will push the limits of your imagination and inspire you to experiment creatively with the patterns.

Right: Satin stitch patterns worked in different ways

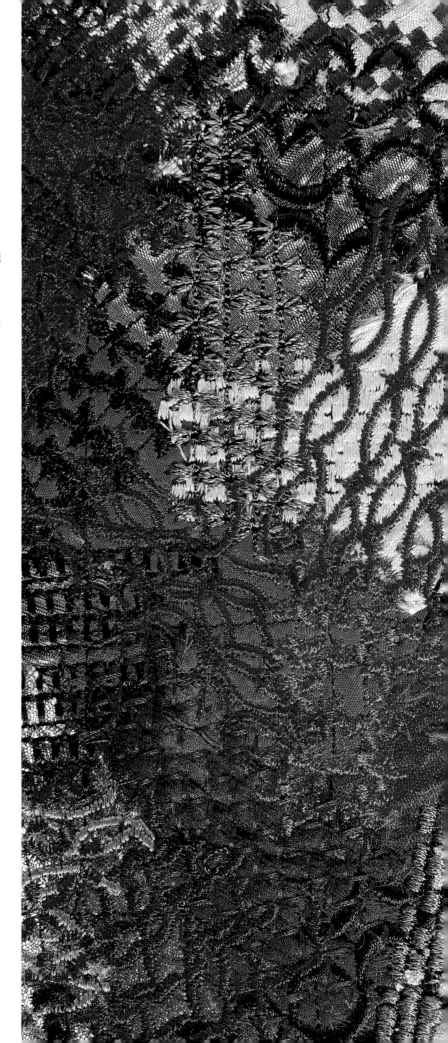

Chapter 1

The Basics

Start with a method:

machine embroidery. Master it.

Begin to look for new applications.

Find them.

Consider the new technologies.

Apply them.

JANET DE BOER

PREPARING TO STITCH

When you first get a new sewing machine, you are probably overwhelmed by the number of controls, knobs and patterns in front of you. The first thing to do is to sit down and work through all the practical stitches and decorative patterns so that you get to know which ones you like. After a while you will also get used to the sound and the feel of the machine, and this is extremely important. Don't plunge in at the deep end by altering the tension, or designing your own patterns – this will wait until later on.

EQUIPMENT

You will need a number of feet, some of which come with the machine and some you may wish to buy as you find a need for them (see pages 11-12). You will also need the usual basic sewing tools, such as scissors, pins, extra bobbins (lots of these) and machine embroidery thread. I also recommend that you get an extra screw for your bobbin case which needs to be partly unscrewed in order to change the bobbin tension. If you go too far and the screw drops out, it is so tiny that you will certainly lose it and your machine is then out of action. And of course this is bound to happen on a Sunday morning!

SETTING UP THE MACHINE

Put the machine on a large table if you can, so there is plenty of space around you for bits of fabric, threads, and tools. Also keep a notebook and pen by you so that you can write down what you have done so that you can repeat the effect.

To check the tension, attach the standard foot, thread a sewing thread through the needle, and use the same thread on the bobbin. Try stitching on two layers of cotton fabric to see whether the stitch locks between the two fabrics. If the bobbin thread shows on the top, either the top thread is too tight or the bobbin thread is too loose. If the top thread shows on the back, then either the top thread is too loose or the bobbin thread is a bit tight. Adjust whichever one is necessary so that normal stitching matches your machine setting. This is usually about 4, or may be indicated by an arrow or a mark showing a standard tension. Fill a number of bobbins before you start to stitch as it is infuriating when the bobbin runs out just as your creative juices are flowing!

NEEDLES

Most swing needle machines and the dedicated embroidery machines such as the Bernette Deco and the Brother PE 100, use the 130/705H needle system. You need a needle with a groove size that fits the thread you are using, so a thicker thread will need a larger needle. Each thread wears the groove in a particular way and so you need to change needles when you change types of thread (from rayon to metallic, for instance), or you will find that the thread starts to shred.

Machine needles are marked in two different sizes, one for Britain and America, and one for Continental countries.

	Very fine			Medium			Very heavy		
CONTINENTAL	60	65	70	75	80	90	100	110	120
BRITISH	8	9	10	11	12	14	16	18	20

Take care when you are using twin needles that the hole in the needle plate is wide enough to accommodate both needles, especially when you are stitching zig-zag stitch or patterns. Some machines will give a warning when this happens or automatically control the width for you.

Fine needles break more often so it is wise to use a standard size of 90 for coloured threads and size 100 (or even 110) for thicker and metallic threads. There are also special embroidery needles available for metal threads, twin needles for making pintucks (in various sizes according to the width of the required pintuck), triple needles for sewing three threads together, wing needles which make an enlarged hole and are excellent for free machining and twin wing needles which have one straight and one wing needle. Ball point needles are used for sewing synthetic fabrics and knits, and jeans needles are designed for use on heavy fabrics.

ALL ABOUT THREADS

Machine embroidery has a very popular following now, and there are the most wonderful variety of machine embroidery threads on the market, which can be bought from specialist embroidery shops, by mail-order, from haberdashery departments in large stores, or from sewing machine shops. These threads are normally made from cotton, rayon or metallic fibres. Machine embroidery threads need to be very strong as they go in and out of the fabric a good many times before the final stitch is made. Buy the 1,000 metre reels, or even large cones if you can, because it is far more economical.

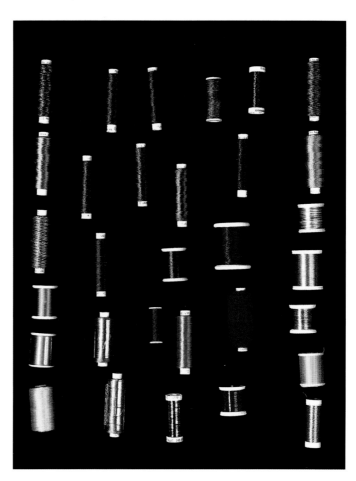

A variety of threads you can use for machine embroidery: rayon, cotton, smooth and textured metallics and variegated colours.

BOBBIN THREAD

If the colour of the thread on your bobbin is not going to show, then you might try using special bobbin thread, bobbinfil, a cheaper overlocking thread, or a mono filament nylon thread on the bobbin. As these threads are fine you can get more on the bobbin which means you do not have to fill it so often. When using whip stitch with the tension altered to show the bobbin thread or cable stitch, and you intend to use the back of the work, you can experiment with other decorative threads. There are metallic threads, or Indian multi-coloured rayon threads, which can be tricky to use as they sometimes shred or break when used through the needle. Heavier threads can be effective when used on the bobbin for cable stitch. The disadvantage of this technique is that you cannot see what you are doing, but you can get a wonderful surprise when you turn the embroidery over.

How some of the patterns will look using thin, medium and thick threads.

TOP THREAD

Use a machine embroidery thread rather than a sewing thread. The embroidery thread is a softer 2-ply thread, with less twist so the fibres lie flatter and reveal more of their gloss. Machine embroidery with a sewing thread, which is a 3-ply thread with a tighter twist, never looks so good, although this is stronger for sewing seams.

Machine embroidery threads come in an enormous range of plain, metallic and textured finishes. They are made in a number of different fibres including cotton, rayon, wool and silk. I think it is rather a waste to use a silk thread as the tiny stitches break up the surface too much and you lose the distinctive lustre of the silk. It is possible to get matt and shiny finishes in other fibres. The threads come in different thicknesses, from 30 (the thickest), to 40, 50, and 60. They are numbered differently from sewing threads so that a 40 machine embroidery thread is quite a bit finer than a 40 sewing thread. The 60 thread is the finest available, but a 40 is the weight that is most commonly used and is available in a range of colours. Some automatic patterns will clog up with thicker threads so you will need to lengthen the stitch, or change the balance control to 'plus' to give the pattern more room.

Machines that work well with finer threads can also be used for combining two threads through the same needle, which is a good way of mixing colours. The thickness of the thread makes a significant difference to the look of the pattern, so experiment to find the one that suits your purpose before you start. The metallic threads come mainly in a single thickness, although there are one or two slightly thicker ones which can be used with care.

THREADING THE MACHINE

On most machines with a horizontal spool pin you should load your reel of thread on the pin with the thread coming from underneath the reel on your side, but check this with your manual. Some small reels have a nick in the rim for holding the thread which can mean

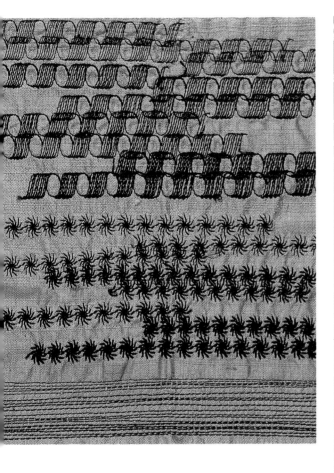

that the thread will catch and break on this while you are stitching, so load the thread away from the tension discs with the nick on the right-hand side.

On machines that hold the thread upright, the thread usually comes from the inner side of the spool next to the machine, but again check with your manual. If you have a problem with the thread bouncing off the reel and getting wound round the spool pin and breaking, try putting a filled bobbin on top to hold it down. Large cones of thread can stand on the table behind the machine, but if you can find a cone guide which holds the thread up in the air above the cone, you will find it will work much better. A piece of wire with a circle bent in one end, stuck into the cone, will also work.

FEET

A selection of feet will come with the machine but you may wish to extend this range as you find a need for them. It would be worth going to your sewing machine dealer and asking for a list of accessories to fit your machine to show you the available options. If there are not very many, or your machine is out-of-date, then you can buy universal feet which will fit any sewing machine (see page 127 for a List of Suppliers). I never begrudge paying for extra feet as they are tailor-made to specific techniques and help you to do the job easily and effectively.

The most useful machine foot is the Satin Stitch, Fancy Stitch, or Embroidery Foot as it

Left: the sample shows the effect of using the finest thread, size 60, the medium ones, sizes 50 and 40, and the thickest, size 30.

Right: other embroidery threads can be wound on the bobbin and the stitching worked upside-down with a loose bobbin tension.

has a wide groove which allows more space for the stitches to pass underneath without ruckling. My next priorities would be the Short-toed Appliqué Foot, a Darning Foot for free embroidery, the Edge Stitcher or Blind Stitch Foot, a Tailor Tacking or Looping Foot (which has a small strip of metal at right angles to the toes which lengthens the stitch between zig-zags and allows you to make a series of loops which give wonderful textures) and an Overedge Foot for solid satin stitch appliqué. All these will be useful to have for the techniques in this book.

Other feet come as extras, and the most useful ones are the Knit Edge Foot (sometimes called the Pearls and Piping Foot, or a Braiding Foot, with a large tunnel underneath it), for making machine-wrapped cords, a Quilting Foot (or Big Foot) for outlining and free embroidery, a Cording Foot for pintucks, and a Braiding Foot for couching and padded satin stitch.

STABILISERS

Any stitching alters the natural structure of a fabric and this often leads to puckering. Massed stitching and condensed stitching, which are obtained when using lines or areas of patterns, cause even more puckering. Thin fabrics are more likely to distort and some, such as twill, rarely do. If your fabric is puckering, first of all try loosening the tension and shortening the stitch length to see if the puckering stops, and then try using one of the various methods for stabilising fabric.

Stabilisers are a great boon to machine embroidery. As well as preventing puckering they make the fabric feed more smoothly through the machine and help prevent skipped stitches. You can use typing paper, tissue paper, disposable nappy liners, or a tear-away backing such as Stitch 'n' Tear to back the fabric while stitching. This can be torn or cut away after you have finished the stitching. I always tear it away after each row of stitching because this is easier than waiting until the end. Then put the Stitch 'n' Tear back under the fabric for the next row and continue in the same way. If the amount of stitching makes it difficult to pull the Stitch 'n' Tear away, try using a gadget for unpicking stitching. You can slide the point of the unpicker

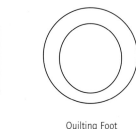

Pattern or Fancy
Stitch Foot

Standard Foot

Braiding Foot

Underneath of
Braiding or Knit Edge
Foot

Darning Foot

Quilting Foot

A selection of some of the most useful sewing machine feet, some of which you will need to buy as extras.

in and rip the stabiliser away from the stitching.

A spray starch can also be used which stiffens the fabric when it is ironed, but after the embroidery is finished, it will wash out. The lighter the fabric, the more starch is needed. Cold water-soluble fabric is a good stabiliser, and can be used underneath or on top. This is useful when the fabric has surface texture or a pile. When you have finished the stitching, hold it under the tap to dissolve the backing. Iron-on Vilene is another excellent stabiliser, but this cannot be removed, so only use it when you are happy with the effect of the resulting stiffness. You can also back a fabric with another fabric such as felt or calico to give stability, and even bond two fabrics together with Bond-a-Web to stiffen them. In extreme cases you can bond two fabrics together and then back them both

with paper – no fabric should pucker with this much stiffening.

For small pieces of stitching you can put the fabric in a hoop, eliminating the need for a stabiliser. Use the largest hoop you can find, but this still means that you can only stitch small areas at one go. Another way to control puckering is to carry on stitching. Masses of stitches will eventually smooth out the puckers and give quite a different handle, creating a fabric which is rich, sensuous, and non-creasing.

You can also take advantage of this puckering and treat it as an asset. By stitching rows of patterns on a fairly fine silk or poly-cotton fabric, the puckering will create an interesting texture, sometimes with a similar appearance to smocking.

Samples showing the use of stabilisers to support fabrics and give them body so they do not cockle when stitched. Some stabilisers can be torn away when the stitching is finished.

TROUBLESHOOTING

Many people do not really understand how sewing machines work. If you take the time and trouble to learn how the stitch is formed and what happens when the needle goes up and down, you will find it much easier to define a problem if anything goes wrong. The following gives an idea of the basic mechanics of the machine:

1   At the start and end of a stitch, the take up lever is fully raised and there is no tension on the thread, so the fabric can move without bending the needle or stretching the thread.

2   As the needle goes down through the fabric, the thread slackens forming a loop. The hook on the bobbin catches the loop and swings it around the bobbin casing. If the top tension is loose, it will form loops the back of the fabric. If it is tight, it will pull the bobbin thread up to the surface. If for any reason the loop fails to form properly, or the bobbin hook fails to catch it, you will get skipped stitches.

Unwanted loops of thread on the top of your fabric mean that the top tension is too tight, or the bobbin tension too loose, or both. Loops on the back of your work mean that the top thread tension is too loose, or the bobbin thread tension too tight, or both.

3   As the needle moves up and down through the fabric, the Presser Foot should hold the fabric firmly. This is not possible if it is too near, or right off the edge of the fabric.

A Darning Foot holds the fabric down firmly at just the time that the needle comes back up.

Here is an outline of common problems, and ways to solve them:

SHREDDED TOP THREAD

◆   Loosen the top tension.

◆   Use a larger needle.

◆   Change the needle – each thread wears the groove of the needle, so thread may shred after it has been changed (for example from rayon to metallic).

◆   If the thread shreds on the last guide, bypass it and go straight through the eye of the needle.

SKIPPED STITCHES

◆   Change your needle – the groove worn by individual threads, or a slightly damaged needle point can cause skipped stitches.

◆   Use a finer needle – for example a size 70 is suitable for use on fine fabrics and jersey fabrics, which have a tendency to cause skipped skitches.

◆   Check that your needle is the right way round, with the flat side to the back.

TOP THREAD KEEPS BREAKING

◆   Try loosening the tension – the tension is often set for a sewing thread, which is usually too tight for embroidery threads. Try using tension 3, 2 or even 1 – the machine will stitch even when the tension is set to nearly 0.

◆   Free the thread if it is catching on the nick of the rim of the thread reel.

◆   Change the needle – the thread may be

shredding on the eye of the needle which has become rough.

- Change to a larger needle – try a size 90 or 100.
- Use an extra thread guide – this will give extra control if the embroidery thread runs wildly off the spool, and winds itself around the spool pin. Alternatively tape a large tapestry needle to the top of the back of the machine which will hold the thread higher than the bottom of the reel.
- Change the thread – the thread may be old or too dry. Central heating can dry out threads so try keeping them in a damper, or cooler room such as the bathroom for a while.

BOBBIN THREAD BREAKS

- Check that the tension is not too tight.
- Make sure the bobbin is wound smoothly – a badly wound bobbin can cause numerous problems.
- Make sure that the bobbin was made by the manufacturer of the machine.

SQUEAKING, GRINDING OR LOUD RUNNING NOISE

- The hook and race probably need oiling – this should be done every four hours of running time. One drop of oil will be enough applied with a paintbrush where the metal bobbin turns against the metal race. This is not appropriate for all machines if the bobbin or bobbin case is made of a different material – check with your manual.

TOUCH SCREEN NOT RESPONDING WELL

- Clean the screen with an anti-static computer screen cleaner – sometimes a thin film of dirt means you have to push quite hard to activate the controls.

COLOURING THE FABRIC

Colouring fabric can have many advantages. You will not need such a big stock of different coloured materials, and it creates a pattern or visual texture on the fabric which adds interest and helps to place the stitching. It is very boring to stitch on a plain piece of fabric without any attempt to colour it, or to build it up with applied pieces of various fabrics. The richer and more interesting the base fabric, the more successful the effect of the stitching will be.

There are many books with details of colouring fabrics using general-purpose fabric paints, silk paints or transfer paints. These paints are readily available and you can just take a brush or small sponge, dip it into the paint and apply it to the fabric in streaks or dabs. The fabric can be wet or dry, and the paints can be diluted with water to give paler colours.

I will only describe methods for colouring fabric here which may not be so well-known:

PAINTING BONDAWEB

Bondaweb is a web of glue backed with paper, generally used for appliqué or to hold layers of fabric together. You iron it on to the back of one fabric before cutting shapes out which will be applied to a second fabric. Then you remove the paper backing. The Bondaweb can feel quite sticky at first, but if left out in the air this stickiness vanishes. You can then decorate it before transferring it to the surface of a fabric.

You can use either silk paints or general-purpose fabric paints. The fabric paints can be used straight out of the jar, or thinned down to give a more watery result and a paler colour. Acrylics can be used but they tend to leave the fabric quite stiff, so use silk paints if possible. Metallic paints tend to act as a resist to the glue, so should be used very thinly and in small quantities.

There are various methods of colouring the Bondaweb:

1   Flood the bondaweb with silk paint, or dilute fabric paint, in different colours, allowing them to flow and mingle with each other.

2   Using quite dry fabric paint straight out of the jar, dab, streak or block print onto the Bondaweb.

3   Allow the paint to flow in runnels or drips by holding a full paintbrush at one end of a piece of Bondaweb held upright, and allowing the paint to run down to the other end. Repeat this using different colours.

4   Trace motifs onto the paper side of the Bondaweb and paint them quite precisely, filling the areas with different colours.

Leave the paint to dry, and then lay it, paint side down, on the top surface of a piece of fabric and iron it off, not forgetting to use a piece of baking parchment both underneath and on top of the sandwich to protect the surface you are using as

well as the iron. You are recommended to use a damp cloth under the iron for maximum 'stick'. You can also peel the coloured web off in strips and lay them, overlapping, on a fabric. Shapes can be cut from the web and laid in a formal pattern or an irregular manner, or strips can be loosely woven with each other. Alternatively you can peel the whole coloured piece off and lay it on the fabric, allowing it to pleat, fold or crunch. Leave the finished fabric out in the air to season which sometimes takes a few days.

You might find that you have to use a Teflon covered foot when stitching painted Bondaweb fabric, depending on what fabric you have used. I have done this when stitching on treated felt, but found there was no need when working on cotton. Watch out for the width of the stitches when working with Teflon feet, as they do not always allow the full width.

BAKED AND GRILLED FABRICS

Baking fabrics turns them into the most wonderful pale to dark caramel colours. I usually start with white or cream fabrics, but those that are already very pale colours, or have been dyed with tea or coffee, also give good results. Silk is particularly successful, but felt, muslin, cotton, velvet, scrim and many papers react very well to this method. Fine fabrics can be gathered in a smock-gathering machine and baked with the threads left in, removing them after drying. Alternatively silk can be pleated or scrunched to leave a textured surface which will never be ironed out no matter how hard you try. Be warned only to bake fabrics when you are alone in the house, as the smell is quite strong, and you will need to air the kitchen afterwards.

BAKED FABRICS

Soak the fabrics for five minutes in hot water, and then squeeze them to remove it. Lay the fabrics on a baking tray in loose balls, and bake them at 200°c/390°F for about 90 minutes.

GRILLED FABRICS

Wet the fabric under the tap, squeeze the water out, and grill at medium heat until it turns the colour you want. You can also splash water onto the fabric during the grilling which will leave interesting marks. Bottled lemon juice flicked onto the fabric will turn brown very quickly under a hot grill. Apply more on top for a darker colour, but do not leave the lemon juice in puddles as it leaves white marks. Try painting marks on the fabric, dipping a brush into the lemon juice and applying it to the fabric before it is grilled.

MARKAL PAINTSTICKS

Markal oil paint sticks come in 53 plain, 12 glitter, 6 fluorescent and 14 irridescent colours, and have the great advantage that they can be used on both paper and fabric. The irridescent paintsticks give a brighter effect than other metallic crayons and are wonderful for bold drawings, and exciting to use on a variety of fabrics.

A skin forms on the surface of the stick which must be rubbed or peeled off before you use it, and the colour can then be rubbed onto the paper or fabric. They are quite soft and are easily blended to give subtle mixes. Markals can be used on any colour background and texture for different effects. They will colour canvas and lace well, and can be used over other fabric paints, or block or potato printed fabrics, to give an extra layer of colour.

Markals can be rubbed on to masking tape, or on to the edges of a stencil or a shape cut from paper. The colour is then rubbed off onto the fabric with a toothbrush to give a soft, shaded effect on the fabric. They can also be used rubbed over string blocks (see page 48), or rubbed directly onto the fabric or over stitching.

Silk, cotton and rayon fabrics after they have been grilled or baked in the oven which gives the caramel colour.

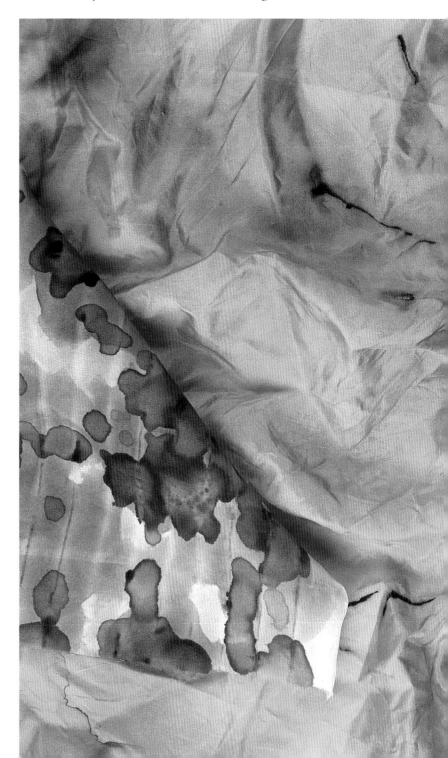

Another method is to rub off some of the colour onto a plate, then pick up the colour using a stencil brush. Hold the stencil firmly and dab the brush onto the fabric through the holes in a stencil until you have deposited enough colour.

Markals will stiffen the fabric slightly, but this is often a good thing anyway. Leave to dry for 48 hours to fix the colour permanently. Then heat set the colour for 10 seconds using an iron set to the highest heat suitable for the fabric you are using. The colour can then take fast to gentle washing.

MAKING STRING BLOCKS FOR RUBBINGS

Draw a design on a piece of paper, or use a photocopy or a computer print out, and glue it to a piece of thick card. The design should be linear, and the lines not too close together. Trim off the edges of the card near the outline of the design, and cover the whole surface with double-sided tape. You can see the design through the tape. Then press lengths of medium to thick string along the lines of the design, leaving out any lines that are confusing, too short, or too close together. Aim for simplicity (see page 48).

As the tape will remain sticky for some time, you can press soft paper or fabric on to the surface and down into the hollows where it will be held while you do the rubbings. Rub the skin off the Markal paint sticks onto some paper. Then rub the paint sticks over the string using one or more colours, until the design is defined. Leave the rubbing out in the air for 48 hours to season. These rubbings can be made on plain paper or fabric, or fabric which has been coloured by some other method, or which is covered with open stitching. This is where practical stitches are

handy, as they texture the surface of the fabric beautifully, and make the rubbing look textured.

DRAWING WITH BOTTLED PAINT

There is a range of fabric paint on the market sold in small bottles with long nozzles. This includes general-purpose fabric paints, metallics, glitter paints and even those that inflate slightly when ironed. They are mostly used for drawing on T-shirts, but are also invaluable for jazzing up a design, adding detail, drawing into stitching to emphasize certain areas, or for adding texture. The long nozzles make them extremely easy to control, and you can leave the lines or dots as they are, or gently smear them to spread the colour. Once dry it is quite possible to stitch over them and into the paint, although it does stiffen the fabric. Apply the paint squeezing the bottle gently, and after drying for 24 hours it will be permanent – no ironing is needed. After 72 hours the fabric can be machine washed or cleaned.

SPRAYING THROUGH STENCILS

Anything with holes in can be used as a stencil, a doiley, a skeletonised leaf, a piece of lace or net, or a card or stencil that you have cut yourself with a sharp knife. You can make your own stencil paper by rubbing a little boiled linseed oil on both sides of a piece of paper and then hanging it up to dry. Build up patterns by cutting out simple shapes using a cutting knife and board.

Place the stencil on a fabric and spray through the holes using either a can of aerosol paint sold for touching up the paint on cars, or fabric paints in plastic bottles with a pump-action spray.

Right: fabric paint sprayed through lace and stencils on different fabrics to build up interesting backgrounds for stitchery.

Chapter 2

Stitched Patterns

Apply the new technologies:

by altering the machine controls, putting different

stitches together, and working on different fabrics,

you can greatly extend the possibilities of even the

simplest stitches.

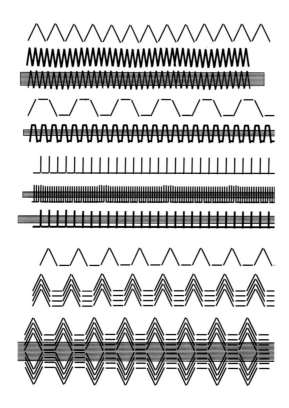

USING STITCHES TO MAKE PATTERNS

Most machines now have some practical stitches and many have decorative patterns as well. Even the most basic stitches can be used decoratively if they are applied with imagination. You can use thicker threads, or two fine threads through the needle to make more impact. You will need a bigger needle to take them, probably a size 90 or 100. The stitch length can be shortened drastically to give a more solid look, or a length of narrow ribbon or strip of fabric can be laid down with the stitch worked on top to give it more impact.

You can even make your own satin stitch patterns by altering the stitch width as you go along and a method for this is included below. Instructions for doing this will often be included in the sewing machine manual. Although a fiddle to do, it does mean that you can achieve a pattern that is not built in to your machine.

MACHINE SETTINGS

Set the width control to the widest stitch possible, which may be 4 on older machines, but 5 or even 6 on the newer ones, and set the stitch length to the satin stitch mark. Work the first few stitches at width 2, then rotate the knob to give width 4 and work a few more stitches. You can count the number of stitches you do each time and with practice you become quite fast and can even do curved patterns. More patterns can be stitched by altering the needle position as well; keeping the needle on one side will give a 'blanket' stitch, while keeping it in the

middle will allow it to swing both sides of the central line.

Produce stitch samples of all the practical and decorative stitches available on your machine using different threads and different fabrics. Don't forget the humble straight and plain zig-zag stitches! The diagram on the machine is not exactly what the stitch will look like on fabric, and it is only by stitching them that you will find out which you like the best, while some may surprise you with unexpected possibilities.

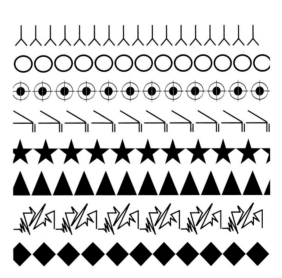

Left: some of the more complex and satin stitch patterns you might find on your machine.

CHANGING THE SETTINGS

Changing the machine settings will alter the look of the built-in patterns, often quite dramatically. The suggestions which follow give an outline of the options open to you.

Right (top): straight bands of stitching worked at different stitch lengths.

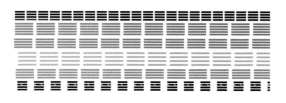

Right (middle): the same stitching worked in bands at right angles to each other giving the effect of weaving.

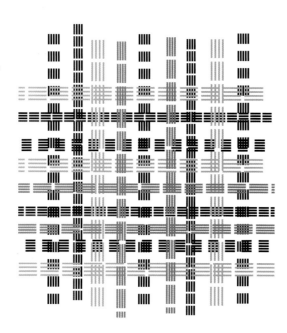

Right (bottom): the same stitching worked as a triangle.

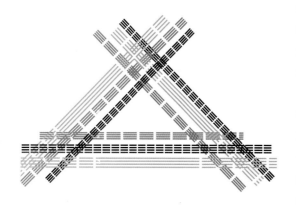

Facing page: samples showing the effect of long and short stitch lengths and the way it alters the tension on the bobbin. The bobbin thread is darker than the top thread and shows more in the shortest stitch length and hardly at all on the longest length.

ALTERING THE STITCH LENGTH

Making the stitch longer or shorter can drastically change the look of a stitch or pattern. If the stitch length is too short, the pattern can clog up, so you will need to experiment for a while to get the best results. No stitch can be too long for any pattern.

ALTERING THE STITCH WIDTH

Working the patterns in a narrow band gives quite a different effect to the same pattern worked at the widest setting. Most machines will not let you decrease the width beyond a certain point and the maximum width is between 7-9mm (¼-⅜in). Newer machines tend to have a greater width. Try stitching bands of the same pattern changing the stitch length, the stitch width, or both together on each row. You will be extremely surprised as you often get quite a different pattern altogether. I spent a long time regretting the sale of an old Bernina which had a particular leaf pattern, only to rediscover it when I lengthened the stitch of quite a different pattern.

USING THE REVERSE BUTTON

As most machines do not sew so well when stitching in reverse, you can use this to break up patterns that are too regular. Just hold the instant reverse button down from time to time, working back over part of the pattern.

CHANGING THE TENSION

If you loosen the top tension to setting 2, or even down to 1, loops of the top thread will appear at the back of the work, giving a variation of whip stitch with much more definition and less regularity. This is usually much more effective than the stitching on the front, so plan it carefully by laying your fabric upside down before you start stitching, or keeping the stabiliser on the top. It is always exciting when you turn the work over and see what has happened.

MAKING PATTERNS BY CHANGING THE STITCH LENGTH OF RUNNING STITCH

You will need a machine with teeth like the Pyrenees and only a few of my machines will do this. Even when it doesn't work you still get a change of tone and colour which makes the visual texture more interesting. With the needle in the fabric you can raise the Presser Foot and turn the fabric without shifting it and this is essential in order to keep the stitches aligned.

First, set your machine to a slightly tighter top tension than is usual for embroidery – about 5. The bobbin tension should be normal. Leave the teeth up and the foot on and set it to straight stitching. Load the bobbin with a strong colour or a variegated thread, and use a shiny or metallic thread through the needle. Set your 'needle down' control. Work a band of straight stitching at stitch length 2, with the lines very close together so that no fabric shows. You do not have to do this perfectly as you can go back and fill in later on. The secret of the whole process is to swivel at the end of each line of stitching with the needle still in the fabric, so that the next row starts in exactly the same place as the previous one stopped.

Then work a band of stitching at stitch length 5, then a band at length 1, then at length 3, and so on. The bands should touch each other to give maximum effect. As the stitch length shortens, the tension tightens and brings the bottom thread up to colour the top thread,

similar to whip stitch but with no loops.

A colour contrast is given to the bands with the longer stitch length, where the shiny thread has the most effect. By working the bands at right angles to each other you will get a woven effect, with a tonal change as you move it around. Try this with two threads through the needle; one metallic and one coloured thread will give quite spectacular results.

ALTERING THE BALANCE OF A PATTERN

The balance controls allow for the fact that stitching behaves differently on different fabrics and makes it possible to match up rows of patterns next to each other on different weights and qualities of fabric. I don't use them in this way, but do alter them to give variations of tone and pattern. These controls are also useful when a pattern 'blocks up', or if you are using a thicker thread which makes the pattern too dense. In either case try adjusting these controls and, if necessary, the stitch length as well.

You will need to experiment with these controls to discover the range of effects. On some machines the minus sign moves parts of the pattern further apart, or works the reverse stitches shorter, and the plus sign moves them closer together or works the reverse stitches longer. On other machines the opposite happens. It is also possible to adjust the sideways movement on large or maxi patterns.

The original feather stitch on the left is varied by altering the length or width of the stitch, or both together, and using the plus and minus balance controls.

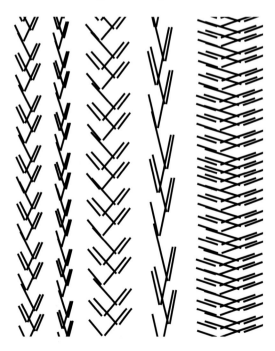

EXPERIMENT TO LEARN THE CONTROLS

Find a notebook, pen and a piece of fabric. Use a stabiliser (a nappy liner will do) and find a thread that is in a contrasting colour to the fabric. Choose a pattern that goes back-and-forth as well as sideways, as this will probably give you the most emphatic differences. Think of what you are doing as a scientific experiment and write everything down in the exact order in which you do it, then you can pin the sample to the paper for future reference. What you will find is that you have a far greater number of patterns than you thought, as the changes can make them look like completely different patterns:

- First row: stitch the pattern as it is set when you choose it
- Second row: stitch the pattern a couple of settings narrower
- Third row: stitch the pattern at the narrowest setting possible
- Fourth row: change the stitch length to the longest possible
- Fifth row: work the pattern at a medium stitch length, but a different one from the first row
- Sixth row: work the pattern at the shortest stitch length
- Seventh row: work the pattern with the balance control set to the highest 'plus' sign
- Eighth row: work the pattern with the balance set to the lowest 'minus' sign

Then stitch some rows putting these together, for example width 6, length 5, and the balance at +7. Do a number of these at different settings. Try a number of border patterns putting some of these rows together. If you like them, follow the instructions in your manual for putting them into the memory, or keep very accurate notes.

Although you will probably work the samples in straight lines, try some of these borders stitched as smooth curves, gently moving the fabric as you stitch. Or you can work overlapping rows to build up gradually darkening tone, or work irregular rows in all directions for more excitement.

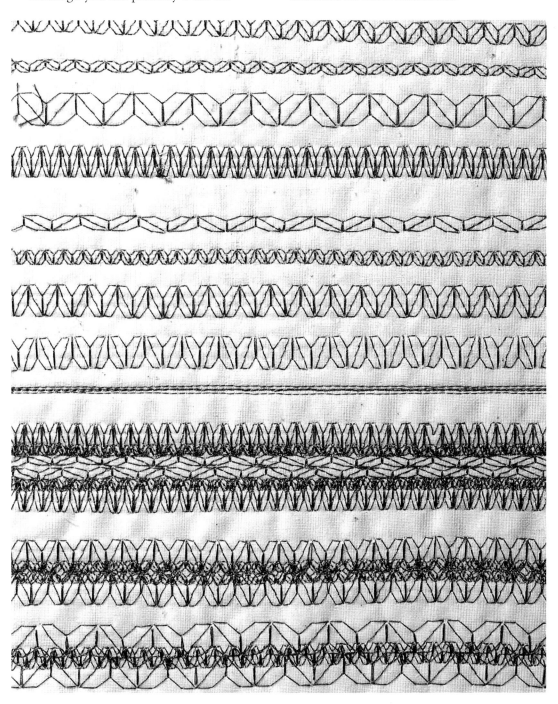

The effect on a single pattern of varying stitch widths, stitch lengths and the plus and minus balance controls.

STITCHING ON DIFFERENT FABRICS

It is valuable to try out different stitch patterns on a range of fabrics such as fine silk where the fabric will probably cockle, muslin where the theads will pull and distort giving a drawn thread effect, felt, sturdy cotton or pelmet vilene where the stitches will stay perfect,

Stitched patterns look entirely different on different fabrics.

velvet where the stitches will squash the pile, or canvas where some of the patterns will distort. You can add all these variations to your list of embroidery techniques. If you stitch on paper it will perforate, so you will need to paint a coat of PVA on the back to strengthen it, or bond the paper to a fabric first using Bondaweb or a spray glue.

If you stitch in black or any other dark-coloured thread on ivory or cream fabric, you will have an effect that looks like blackwork done by hand. If you stitch open patterns or the practical stitches using a toning coloured thread on a painted fabric, you will achieve a textured fabric with a nice feel and more body than the original fabric. If you stitch on velvet and flatten the pile, your stitches (even if they are brightly coloured) will hardly show from certain angles and reveal colourful flashes as you move the piece around. If you wish to change the ground fabric even more, you can pull threads, cut slits, burn or punch holes, gather or shirr it or fold or pleat it before starting to stitch.

We all have collections of small scraps of fabrics, kept because we might need them some time, and now is a good time to get them out and play with them. You can apply small pieces or long strips of other fabrics, perhaps shiny ones on a matt fabric, or transparent pieces to change the colour. Try some unexpected combinations like organza laid over canvas, scraps of brightly coloured cottons between layers of plastic bag, or small pieces of gathered fabric laid on a smooth one. If you find they move while you stitch, you might have to tack the pieces by hand before machining.

SATIN STITCH PATTERNS

Most machines come with a few satin stitch patterns, even if they only include small scallops for edging and the top models have a very large range. Some machines offer a system of individual satin stitch shapes such as diamonds or ovals which you can put together to make quite complex patterns, and then store them in the memory of the machine. In the early days of zig-zag machines, the instruction books used to tell you how to devise your own patterns manually by altering the needle position and the width of the satin stitch. This seems like an awful lot of hard work, but if you set your machine to satin stitch at the widest width and alter the width setting every few stitches you will make some quite interesting patterns. Counting the stitches in between the width changes was advised, but that is too much for those of us spoilt by automation, so if you do it at random it will result in a much freer effect.

MACHINE SETTINGS

Try samples of different stitch lengths for each satin stitch pattern to see which gives the best stitch density (just close enough to make solid shapes, but not so close that the stitches pile up on each other). The width should be set as wide as possible to make the most of the pattern, but of course try different widths just to find out what happens.

The look of satin stitch patterns will change according to the thickness of the thread you are using. If the thread is thicker, say a size 30, you will probably find that the patterns pile up on each other and you will need to lengthen the stitch. Or, if you are using a fine size 60 thread,

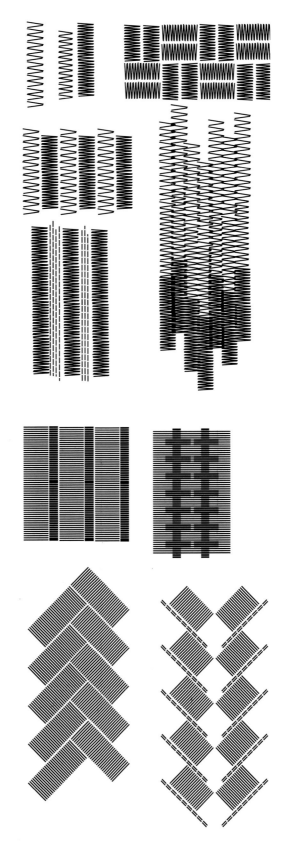

Left (top): satin stitch and zig-zag used together to make patterns and giving tonal changes.

Left (bottom): some of the patterns you can make using blocks and bands of satin stitch.

there will be too much spacing between the stitches and you will need to shorten the stitch length. This can take you by surprise, so remember to adjust the stitch length rather than thinking that there is something wrong with the machine. The quality of fabric you are stitching on and whether or not you are using a stabiliser will also make a difference. Machine patterns are effective when worked on a stable, firm fabric so it is necessary to strengthen more flimsy fabrics to achieve a perfect pattern. (See stabilising fabric pages 12-13).

CORNERS

Corners can be problematic to stitch accurately in satin stitch. If possible avoid doing a perfect or mitred corner by crossing over at the corners, or by butting them. If you want perfect corners, then start a pattern at the point of a corner and stitch away from it. Then come back to the point, set your machine to the beginning of the pattern and stitch the other way. You may have to leave a gap in the centre of the band as the pattern is unlikely to join perfectly in the middle.

Another possibility is to stitch to within half an inch or so of the corner and then do straight satin stitch until the corner, turn, do another length of satin stitch to match, and then start the pattern again. Alternatively you could diagonally bisect the corner.

Complex and multiple patterns are impossible to match perfectly at the corners as each pattern is a different length. One way around the problem is to stitch straight lengths on strips of fabric and mitre the corners by turning them back or cutting them on the diagonal and applying them to a ground fabric. If you have cut them, then you will need to cover the join with a decorative stitch or plain satin stitch and this becomes part of the design. Do this repeatedly and you can make chevron and triangular patterns.

Right (top): some of the ways you can devise good looking corners when using satin stitch patterns.

Right (bottom): a scrolling satin stitch pattern worked over the top of a more open herringbone type stitch.

Far right: a number of different satin stitch patterns worked in different ways: in straight rows, in blocks in different directions, and in layers.

INDIVIDUAL PATTERNS

The ability to stop automatically at the end of a stitch pattern is a great bonus when you want to combine elements from different patterns, or to stitch a 'spot' pattern with scattered motifs all over a surface. You push the single pattern key, or choose the icon on the screen and click on it, and the machine will stitch one section of a pattern starting with a couple of stitches on the spot and finishing off the thread at the end with another few stitches on the spot. The little outline patterns are not suitable for this, but the satin stitch patterns, or sections of them, are ideal. On some machines there are larger patterns, usually meant for decorative edges, but which individually make a larger mark on your fabric.

They can give a very rich texture when repeated at different angles, and overlapping, or used in lines they can make interesting borders.

Start by selecting one section of a pattern and storing it in the memory. Mirror the selection, store that too, then change direction and rotate the motif and store that in the memory – and so on. This is a simplified version and you will have to check your manual for more detailed instructions on how to use this method. Overall it saves you an enormous amount of time and makes it unnecessary to keep stopping and starting the machine and moving the fabric and cutting the threads between each motif.

These small 'spots' or motifs are quite enchanting and can be used overlapping each other to build up rich texture (for example spot quilting through layers of fabrics and wadding), or to make an all-over, random, spot pattern as a basis to build on with richer stitching or borders. They can be outlined with hand stitchery, for example fly stitch around a satin stitch diamond or triangle, or they can be overstitched with cross or straight stitches.

You can also use a section of a pattern, such as a triangle, and mirror and rotate it, putting each change into the memory of your machine, to stitch a larger pattern without endlessly moving the fabric. You can also use the directional facility on the machine to move the triangle further down the fabric, or at an angle.

Individual patterns worked informally, with zig-zag and satin stitch bands suggesting ways of using them in landscapes.

Left: some combinations of individual satin stitch triangles built up to make more complex patterns. They have been rotated and moved, and stored in the memory of the sewing machine.

Below: individual sections used randomly over painted fabric, openly and massed.

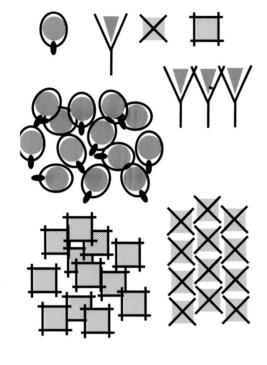

Right (top): blocks of satin stitched individual patterns, outlined and emphasised with hand stitchery.

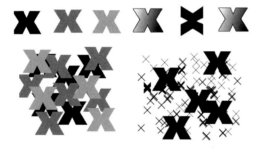

Right (opposite and below): individual patterns used over narrow ribbons, hand stitchery such as running or cross stitch, or building up rich areas of texture by working the stitches on top of each other using different coloured threads.

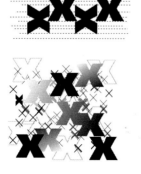

Far right: bands of satin stitched patterns cut into short lengths and stitched together again, with the back of the stitching showing alternately with the front.

COMBINING PATTERNS

The built-in patterns on older sewing machine models can be only 4mm (⅛in) wide, and on newer ones often still only 5 or 6mm. Pfaff machines offer 9mm (⅜in) wide patterns but this is still too narrow to make much visual impact. You can get round this by doing multiple rows of the same or different patterns. If you choose two or three practical stitches or open embroidery patterns the results will look fairly thin, so you can lay down a narrow ribbon or strip of fabric, or a length of knitting ribbon or yarn while you are stitching the pattern to give it more strength. If you have satin stitch patterns on your machine then you can use these to give greater strength to the design, but they often look better when edged, or alternated, with an open pattern to blend it into the background fabric. You can, of course, use a thicker thread, perhaps a size 30, but be aware that the pattern may clog up and you might need to change the stitch length or use the balance controls to rectify this.

WHIP STITCH

If you loosen the bobbin tension, tighten the top tension, or do both, you will get a whip stitch, with the bobbin thread coming up to the surface, which gives the stitch a stronger line. If you want a more delicate version of the pattern, then keep the top thread the same colour as the fabric, put the contrasting colour thread on the bobbin and work whip stitch so that delicate flecks of bobbin thread colour make a less strongly defined pattern. I am very fond of working sometimes from the front and sometimes from the back of a fabric to give changes of tone and colour. I find this way of working prevents too mechanical a look – this is especially effective with a variegated thread.

MACHINE SETTINGS

Set the top tension to about 6, or higher if you are using a strong thread. Slightly loosen the bobbin thread by turning the bobbin case screw slightly anti-clockwise. Try this out on a spare piece of fabric before you use it on your embroidery as you might need to tighten the top tension a bit more. If you have do not want to alter your bobbin tension, then loosen the top tension down to about 2 or 3, and work upside-down. The top thread will then go through to the back and make tiny loops underneath the fabric.

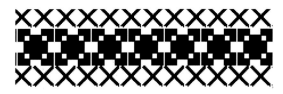

Some satin stitch patterns combined with more open patterns to contrast with each other.

Right (top): a complex border using bands of stitches combined with individual segments of satin stitch patterns.

Right (middle): loosening the bobbin tension so that loops of thread come to the surface, gives a whip stitch. Working patterns in whip stitch produces more texture and can be worked on the front or the back of the fabric.

Facing page and below: open and densely stitched patterns worked in bands, irregularly in blocks, and in a grid pattern.

CABLE STITCH

By putting a thicker thread on the bobbin you can use cable stitch on the pattern by working from the back of the fabric. Satin stitch patterns cannot be done like this as the thread is too thick. However the practical stitches and open patterns are fine when worked in cable stitch, and give lovely strong patterns. The only drawback is that you have to keep changing the bobbin as the thread runs out more quickly. Some reels of thread, such as perlé, can be wound by threading it through the bobbin winding path, and then holding the reel on a pencil while it is being wound. Others, such as 4-ply knitting wool, you might have to wind onto the bobbin by hand (which you can do while you are watching television!).

MACHINE SETTINGS

Loosen the bobbin tension so that the thicker thread pulls through smoothly. Leave the top tension normal.

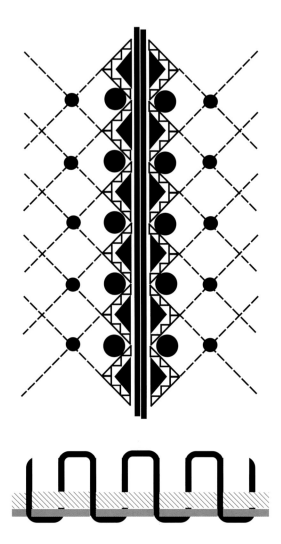

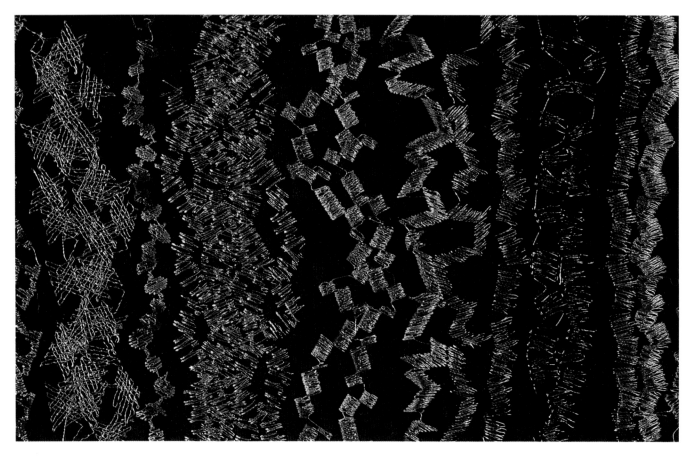

Above: sample of a number of different stitches worked swinging the fabric from side to side. Gold thread was used through the needle, and a variegated thread in the bobbin, worked with a loose bobbin tension so the thread comes to the top of the fabric.

Facing page: an automatic feather stitch type pattern worked over scraps of bonded fabrics, swinging the fabric from side-to-side while stitching.

SWINGING STITCHES

It is quite easy to do fairly free embroidery without removing the foot or dropping the teeth or using a frame for the fabric. Just gently guide the fabric in any direction you wish. You can swing from side-to-side, move the fabric in a random way, or even go round in circles or spirals. You will need a large enough piece of fabric to hold on to with both hands as you move it around, and if the fabric is thin or stretchy, you will probably need two layers or a stabiliser.

MACHINE SETTINGS

Set your machine to one of the practical stitches or an embroidery pattern, leave all the tensions

and settings as normal, and then stitch while you are swinging the fabric. Sometimes there will be gaps between the stitches and sometimes they will overlap, but you will achieve lovely free effects. These would look wonderful on an embroidery of a garden or landscape, could represent animal markings, or look like the movement of water. I have also made some pieces using this stitch to give the impression of undergrowth, or stubble in a field after the harvest.

As this method is quite difficult to control on a small scale, I suggest that you work areas of these textures and then cut them out and apply them to a backing ready for further hand or machine stitching.

Facing page: freely stitched automatic patterns worked while moving the fabric in a regular scallop or vermicelli pattern.

Right (top): these satin stitch pattern settings will give you the best results when worked in free movements.

Right (bottom): move your frame in scallops or in vermicelli patterns while the machine is set to one of the previous patterns.

FREELY STITCHED AUTOMATIC PATTERNS

Doing free machine embroidery with the machine set on one of the automatic patterns can lead to some unexpected results. The needle will dart about in different directions, but just ignore this and concentrate on moving your framed fabric in a regular pattern, or randomly if you prefer. Start with the built-in satin stitch patterns such as scallops, ovals, hearts and so on, as patterns with an even width of stitch, such as chevrons, are not so effective. Vary the background fabric, the top tension and the colour of the thread to give different effects.

MACHINE SETTINGS

The top tension on your machine should be set either to normal, or slightly looser. Frame the fabric tightly, and use the Darning Foot, Quilting Foot or Big Foot if you can (otherwise take the foot off altogether). Then drop the teeth (the feed dog), choose a pattern and start stitching, running the machine fast, and moving the frame very slowly to allow the satin stitch to build up in some areas.

You can work another layer of this stitching on top in a different coloured thread to give an even richer pattern and texture. Try a metallic pattern over a coloured one, or a dark thread over a pale one, as there should be a contrast in either tone or colour for this to work. If you tighten the bobbin slightly, and loosen the top tension to about 1 or 2, you will have both colours of threads showing on the back, and there will be more texture, so plan to use this and place your fabric upside-down in the frame. The varied colour breaks up the pattern,

expecially if you are using a variegated thread either through the needle or in the bobbin, as this adds even more colour interest.

Altering the fabric you are stitching on can be most effective. Try bonding strips or scraps of different fabrics, wisps of variegated silk or nylon tops (unspun 'fleece') to a base fabric. Try stitching on a strongly patterned fabric to blend the colour and shapes, a fabric which you have block printed or painted, or on top of previously stitched bands of automatic stitches.

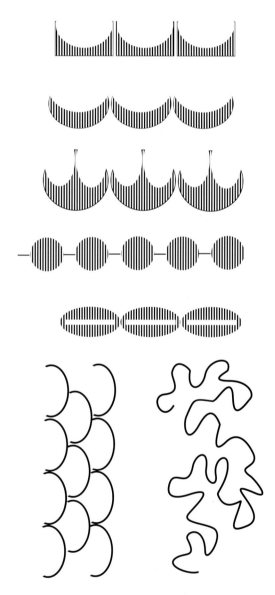

OUTLINED PATTERNS

Individual patterns, parts of patterns or rows of patterns can be outlined to make them stronger and more interesting. This involves using free machine embroidery which gives a less regimented look to the pattern, and makes it more individual. If you stitch with the top tension loose on 3 (or even two or minus on some machines), the back of the stitching will often become more exciting.

FREE RUNNING OUTLINES

Stitch the pattern in the middle of a piece of fabric. Then set the machine for free embroidery by dropping the feed dog and putting the Darning Foot on to replace the Presser Foot. Put the stitched fabric in a ring frame and stitch outlines round the pattern moving the frame slowly. Don't sew too close to the pattern and press hard on the foot control to run the machine at high speed. This gives you more control than when you run at slow speed, which can also give an angular look to the stitches. Individual motifs can also be outlined, along with the larger patterns that come with some machines.

WHIP STITCH OUTLINES

Stitch the pattern in the middle of a piece of fabric and set the machine for free embroidery by dropping the feed dog, putting the Darning Foot on and the stitched fabric in a ring frame. Loosen the bobbin tension slightly and fill a couple of bobbins with a decorative thread. Use transparent nylon thread or a strong embroidery thread through the needle. Tighten the top thread slightly and work whip stitch outlines outside the patterns. Again, press hard on the foot control to run the machine at high speed and move the frame slowly. Do not worry about making small mistakes as inaccuracies can enrich the effect of the pattern.

SATIN STITCH OUTLINES

Stitch the pattern in the middle of a piece of fabric and set the machine for free embroidery by dropping the feed dog, putting the Darning Foot on and the stitched fabric in a ring frame. Set the stitch to zig-zag, on approximately width 2, and work a line of satin stitch curving around one side of a segment of the pattern. Then cross over to the other side and work a second line. Keep the frame the same way up so that the width of the line changes as you stitch, rather like using a calligraphic pen. You could then do a return journey filling the other side of the pattern, leave it as it is, or do two or more lines on one side only.

Machines will sew better going forwards than backwards, particularly when sewing satin stitch, so try to always start from the top and work downwards.

Bands of pattern and individual motifs outlined with free running, whip or narrow satin stitch, worked with the Darning Foot on and dropped teeth.

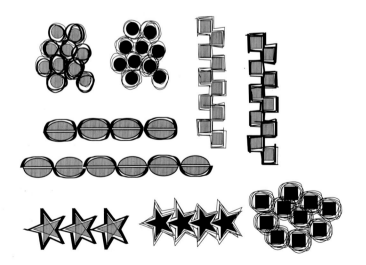

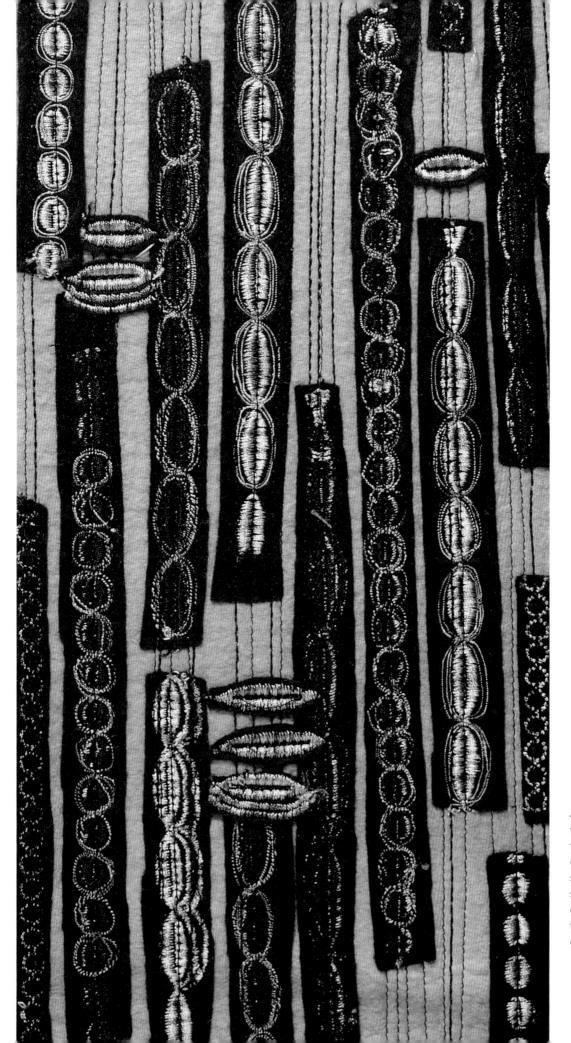

A satin stitch pattern
worked on the back and
the front of the fabric
outlined with running
stitch and narrow satin
stitch. The patterns were
cut into strips and applied
to a baked fabric with lines
of straight stitching.

Chapter 3

Fabrics & Patterns

Begin to look for new applications:

You can use the machine patterns to decorate, and

even make, fabrics which are totally unique.

Right: some of the
patterns that work well
when used for quilting.
Denser patterns take
forever and are often too
rigid for this purpose.

QUILTING WITH PATTERNS

Machine quilting can look rigid, particularly when it is done in straight lines so that it loses the lovely softness of hand quilting. However if you use one of the practical stitches or an open automatic pattern, it will have a distinctive, quilted effect of quite a different quality to hand quilting.

For simple quilting, you can stitch one of the patterns in diagonal lines, about 2-2½cm (¾-1in) apart, all over a fabric sandwich with a backing fabric such as cotton, a wadding, and a top fabric. If you use a Walking Foot, which is sold as an extra, or the Dual Feed Foot on the Pfaff, you hardly need to tack the layers together – a few pins will be all that is needed, unless the piece you are stitching is fairly large. Maybe you can find a fabric with a large pattern on it to use as a guideline for the stitching, or you can print your own fabric with a suitable design. Keep to straight lines or gentle curves, and make sure they are not too close together or you will loose the soft effect that is so essential to quilted work.

If you choose a transparent fabric, then you can place strips or cut shapes of other fabrics underneath to build up a pattern to stitch round. It will also look more interesting when you are just stitching in diagonal rows.

Spot quilting, similar to tied quilting, uses separated knotted stitches all over the surface and can be easily stitched using individual motifs either placed at random or in a defined pattern. Because the machine stitches on the spot at the beginning and the

end of each motif or section, the stitching is quite firm even when you have cut off all the threads.

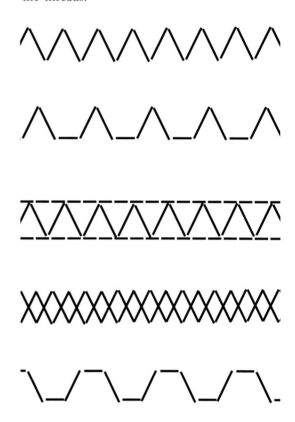

MACHINE SETTINGS

Keep the machine tensions normal, and use the Embroidery Foot or Walking Foot. Depending on the design of your machine you need to either tap the single pattern key or button, or click that setting on the screen.

For continuous lines of quilting choose one of the more open patterns (otherwise you will be stitching endlessly) set at about width 3. I should choose one of the satin stitch patterns for the spot quilting as the open patterns will hardly show up at all. You could use one of the larger built-in patterns if your machine has one, otherwise choose a shape such as a satin stitch diamond, or tiny flower.

Facing page: a
commercially patterned
organza, backed with strips
of transparent fabrics,
quilted along the lines of
the patterns with an open
pattern, and spot quilted in
the centre with satin stitch
squares.

STITCH FIRST – THEN QUILT

If you stitch all over a piece of fine cotton or other fabric using a zig-zag, herringbone or one of the overlocking stitches, it will give body to the fabric and a lovely texture. You can use the same coloured thread or a contrasting one, but I like using a similar colour thread, such as navy on black, and then placing the fabric over a string block and doing a rubbing using Markal oil sticks. (See pages 17-18). Then quilt it using a contrasting thread and a different stitch. Alternatively do the all-over stitching and lay the fabric over a backing and a layer of wadding. Using a contrasting colour thread, either stitch in rows using one of the patterns or use spot quilting.

Right (top): a flower drawn from a piece of Turkish embroidery used as the design for the string block.

Right (bottom): block made of string glued to card. The stitched fabric was placed on top of the card and the pattern rubbed with Markal paint sticks. Free running stitch in gold thread outlined the pattern and quilted it at the same time.

QUILTING WITH STITCHING AND SLASHING

A different quilting method involves stitching through four, five or six layers of fabrics where the top layers are slashed to reveal the backing. After cutting and stitching the fabric is washed in the washing machine and dried in a tumble drier to make it soft and fluffy. This fabric is very supple with a rich texture, particularly when using muslin.

QUILTING WITH PATTERNS

Normally the fabrics are stitched together with parallel lines of straight stitches, because two lines of stitches are needed fairly close together to secure the fabric. I find that stitching a narrow pattern such as a herringbone pattern or one of the practical stitches, is more effective. It is better to slash the fabric on the bias so that it does not fray, so if you are going for horizontal or vertical lines of slashing either

use the fabric on the bias or stitch on the diagonal. If you stitch the fabric on the straight of the horizontal or vertical grid, then you can use the fabric on the straight of the grain as the cuts will be on the diagonal.

Pin the layers of fabric together, using a dark, strong, fabric for the backing. This has to support all the other layers, as well as acting as a lining. You can use very contrasting colours for these fabrics as they will show after you have cut them, but keep the thickest fabric near the bottom as it will not bend so far when it is slit. Fine cotton, rayon or silk fabrics all work well, but velvet is a bit too thick. The top fabric can be patterned, painted or sprayed, or you can use strips or squares of different coloured fabrics. Experiment with the fabrics in different orders, as the results are often unexpected. Do not prewash the fabrics, as a bit of shrinkage makes the final texture more pronounced.

Layers of fabrics stitched with bands of patterns and slashed to show the fabrics underneath.

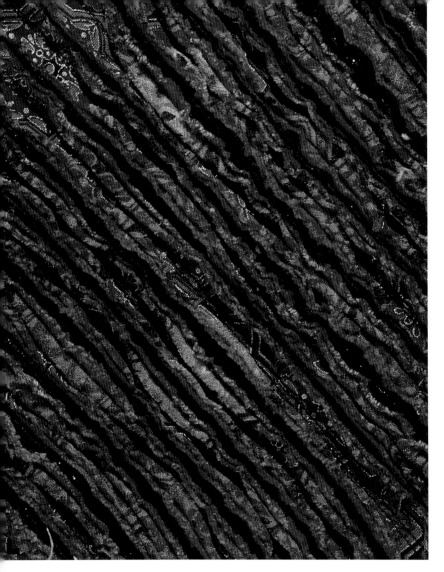

Above: layers of fabric secured with a narrow stitched pattern, slashed between the stitching above.

Right (top): stitched patterns worked through layers of fabric. The dotted lines indicate where the slashing will be.

Far right: groups of stitched lines, with slashes between them, can build up patterns like this.

MACHINE SETTINGS

Try setting the stitch pattern at width 2, and use the same, or a darker coloured thread as the fabric. Stitch in parallel lines, about 1½-2cm (½-¾in) apart, or in a grid pattern, using the edge guide which screws in to a hole in the back of the sewing foot holder. Carefully slit the fabrics between the stitching using fine, sharp scissors. It looks somewhat stiff at this stage, so needs to be 'wrecked' to soften it and make the texture more interesting. Do this by putting the quilted piece in your washing machine and take it through the complete cycle. If you have a tumble dryer, then put it in this for about half an hour at a low setting. Otherwise, dry it outside on a windy day, roughing it up between your hands every so often.

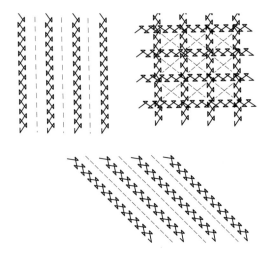

QUILTING WITH BLOCKS OF PATTERNS

A second method of quilting layers of fabrics is to stitch bands of patterns at different angles. Place these either randomly or in a regular pattern. Use large, open patterns contrasting with some satin stitch patterns, leaving spaces between the blocks of stitching. Fill these with lines of running stitch about ½cm (¼in) apart as a contrast to the pattern. If you wish to slash between the lines, stitch them 1½cm (½in) apart, and work two rows of stitching very close together to hold the fabrics secure.

MACHINE SETTINGS

Leave the tensions as normal, but use the widest stitch possible to make the best use of the patterns.

Patterns and Ribbons

Layers of ribbons of different widths and colours, enriched with lines of embroidery patterns, make very rich braids. These can be used to trim clothes, or laid in rows on a fabric, with lines of further stitching between them, to make a richly decorated fabric suitable for use on cushions, small bags or book covers.

The trick is to find the ribbons in the right colours and textures for your purpose, and it is best to look for the satin, taffeta and woven ribbons. The transparent ribbons are slightly too fragile, and velvet is usually too thick and moves about too much while you are stitching. Choose a wide ribbon for the base of the braid, then one that is slightly narrower, then a fine one, or two very fine ribbons. Tack them together so they do not slip while they are being stitched.

Machine Settings

Keep both thread tensions normal, or loosen the top tension if necessary so that the bobbin thread does not show on the top. If it shows on the back, it does not matter because the braid will eventually be laid on top of a fabric. Use the Satin Stitch or Embroidery Foot for most of the stitching.

Using a toning thread, stitch a line of running stitch right down the centre to keep all the layers together. If you like the look of this running stitch, then work some more rows, choosing a contrasting thread which will add body to the braid. Then choose a satin stitch pattern and add the decoration. The edges of the ribbons will have started to flute, and need more running stitches to straighten them out. This can be tricky, so put the Edging Foot on your machine to keep your lines of stitching parallel and close to the edge of the ribbon.

Left: layers of ribbons with automatic patterns and running stitch.

Below: stitched and beaded ribbons which can be used to decorate clothes, bags and cushions.

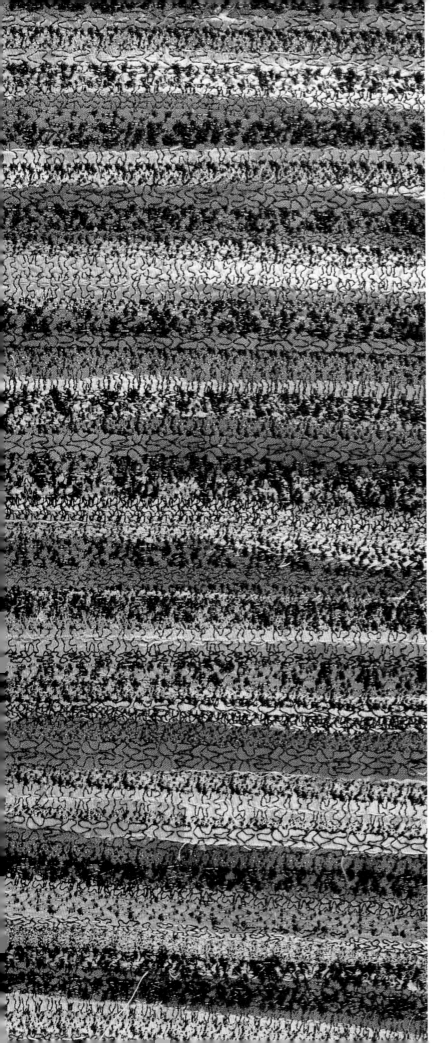

Decorating a Fabric

The most unique and exciting fabrics can be made by stitching a plain or patterned fabric all over with bands of decorative stitches. The trick is to find which stitches look the best by themselves or in combinations when stitched all over the surface. The patterns should be worked as wide as possible and often look good when a solid pattern is placed next to a more open or delicate one. Even plain zig-zag can look wonderful, and you could start by experimenting with this stitch. The fabrics made this way are quite stiff and are good for use as bags, belts, straps, book covers, or decorative elements on clothes.

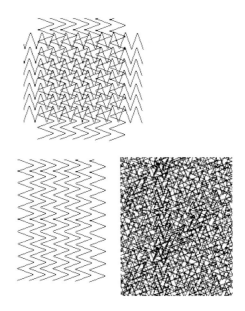

Machine Settings

Choose a suitable fabric – perhaps a thickish cotton – and a stabiliser. Set the machine at normal tension top and bottom, with the teeth up and the Satin Stitch or Embroidery Foot on.

Firstly, stitch a fabric with bands of stitches all in the same direction and the lines nearly

touching each other. You can use a plain or variegated thread, and if one of the colours of the variegated thread is the same as the fabric colour, you will lose the pattern every so often, which makes it look less regular. Then try another sample using two layers of stitches with the second layer going at right angles to the first. Then do a third sample with the third layer on the diagonal and the fourth layer in the opposite direction. This uses four layers of stitching in total and each layer could be a different colour thread. If you work the diagonal layers first and the vertical and horizontal ones on top, the effect will be different again.

Now try some of the stitch patterns over bonded strips of mixed fabrics, or cut out shapes bonded to a base fabric. Or take a strip of fabric and fold it randomly back and forth on the ground fabric as you stitch. Try working rows of the same or different patterns using different stitch lengths and widths. One effect I am

particularly fond of is created by working both on the back and front of the fabric with a slightly loose top tension, so that the stitching looks dense in some places and delicate in others.

These fabrics can be used as they are, or cut up into smaller shapes and stitched together again rather like crazy patchwork, or used in narrow strips to build up really textured backgrounds for other embroidery.

Above: the decorated fabrics cut into strips and stitched to a backing fabric.

Left: some pattern combinations which can be used to decorate fabrics.

Facing page (left): lines of zig-zag stitching worked in different directions, building up layers of colour and texture.

Facing page (far left): fabrics applied to a backing, decorated with rows of automatic patterns on the front and back.

PATTERNS AND APPLIQUÉ

We are quite accustomed to idea of machine appliqué and both the practical stitches and the embroidery patterns can be used to apply one piece of fabric to another. If the shapes are curved or complex they should be quite large or it will be difficult to stitch around them easily. Straight sides are much easier to start with, so choose strips, squares or diamonds for your first sample. As you stitch you might push the fabric edge forward somewhat, so it is better if the shapes are bonded onto the backing fabric first to avoid this.

Right: two or three decorated fabrics can be used together to make patterns – this shows different shapes cut from each one, laid on a backing fabric ready to stitch down.

Right (bottom): a decorated fabric can be cut into shapes and laid on a backing fabric ready for stitching.

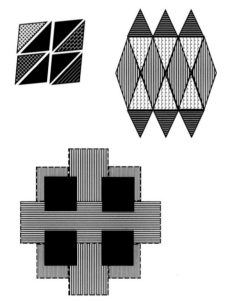

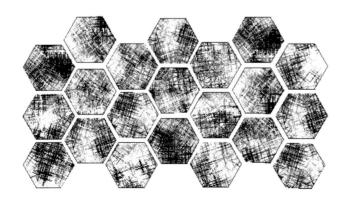

The idea of applying pieces of stitched fabric to another fabric is less widely used but it is even easier to do because it has more body than an unstitched fabric and will not cockle or move so easily. Therefore a piece of stitching does not need bonding, but can be just pinned to the background.

MACHINE SETTINGS

Keep both tensions normal, the foot up and use the Satin Stitch Foot. If you have a Pfaff and are applying fairly simple shapes use the Dual Feed Foot, which prevents the top piece from slipping. If you have another machine, you will be able to attach a separate Walking Foot. Do not use a thread thicker than 40 because the satin stitches will clog up.

Wonderfully rich patterns can be made by cutting up two or three different decorated fabrics and placing them next to each other, securing them with satin stitched edges or satin stitch patterns. If you wish for a more supple result, then leave spaces between the pieces which can be decorated with further rows of patterns.

Try making log cabin type patterns, starting with a square in the centre and stitching strips of embroidered fabrics around it, edging them with satin stitch in a contrasting colour. Then when it is finished, cut it up again into strips or squares and move them around to make a new pattern. More satin stitching covers the cut edges and secures them to the background. Any patchwork type pattern can be built up in this way, and the added firmness of the piece makes it excellent for the centres of cushions or for bags, belts, book covers or even luggage.

 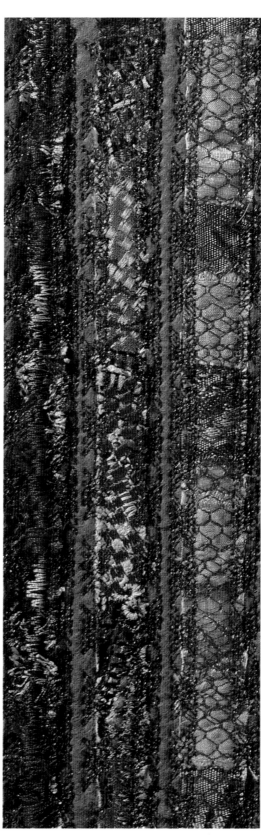

Left and far left: plain or decorated fabrics cut up and applied to a backing using automatic patterns on the edges, or secured with multiple lines of triple straight stitch.

Right (top): a log cabin pattern, built up of strips of fabric decorated with bands of patterns.

Right (bottom): the log cabin pattern cut up and rearranged to make a new pattern.

Left (top): strips of decorated fabrics placed together making a log cabin pattern. Start with the central square, and gradually work outwards with longer and longer strips. Stitch along all the joins with satin stitch.

Left (bottom): drawing of an African figure which could be cut out in fabric and applied to a background fabric, building up border patterns.

DISTORTED PATTERNS

Machine patterns can be stitched on hot or cold water-soluble fabric or vanishing muslin. Once the fabric is dissolved only the stitching remains, distorted, uneven and beautifully lacy. Stitch overlapping rows of patterns, making sure that the stitching interlocks otherwise the whole piece will come to bits when the fabric has dissolved. If you have any doubts, go back and work a few more rows over the weaker areas. Both the top and bottom threads will show in the final embroidery, and it is very effective if these contrast, perhaps using one coloured thread and one metallic. The stitching can be done in straight or curved lines, as a grid, or swinging the stitches around to make less formal patterns. You may find that more holes appear after the fabric is dissolved than you thought would be there. I find this unexpectedness a bonus and like the continual surprises that appear. Another option is to apply small lacy bits to another decorated fabric. Alternatively you can put them back onto water-soluble fabric and add more stitching to build up layers and make a complete fabric in its own right.

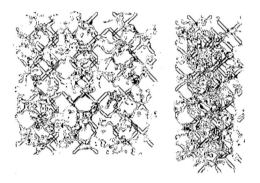

HOT WATER-SOLUBLE FABRIC

Any good embroidery thread will withstand the boiling needed to dissolve the hot water-soluble fabric (I have done extensive tests with nearly every thread sold today and have had no trouble at all). This fabric looks like organza, is very easy to stitch on to and although it will pucker, the puckers will dissolve. When the work is finished, cut away any excess fabric (which can be saved and stitched roughly together again to use another time) and plunge the embroidery into boiling water. The reaction happens terribly quickly as the stitching rolls up into a small ball and it seems to be lost forever. Leave it in for about 30 seconds, moving it about with a wooden spoon. Lift the embroidery out with wooden tongs and plunge into cold water. If it still feels slightly slimy it means that traces still remain in the fabric. Put it back into the simmering water again to rinse it completely, or leave if you prefer the fabric to dry stiffly.

COLD WATER-SOLUBLE FABRIC

This fabric looks like soft plastic and is much cheaper. It is not always quite so easy to stitch on, but using a ballpoint needle or a Teflon Foot improves this. The disadvantage

Right (bottom): pattern stitched on water-soluble fabric, in even bands or randomly.

Right (top): how it would look after the fabric is dissolved.

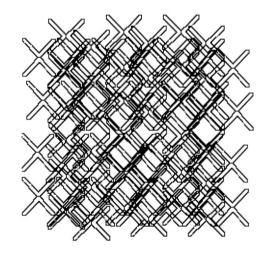

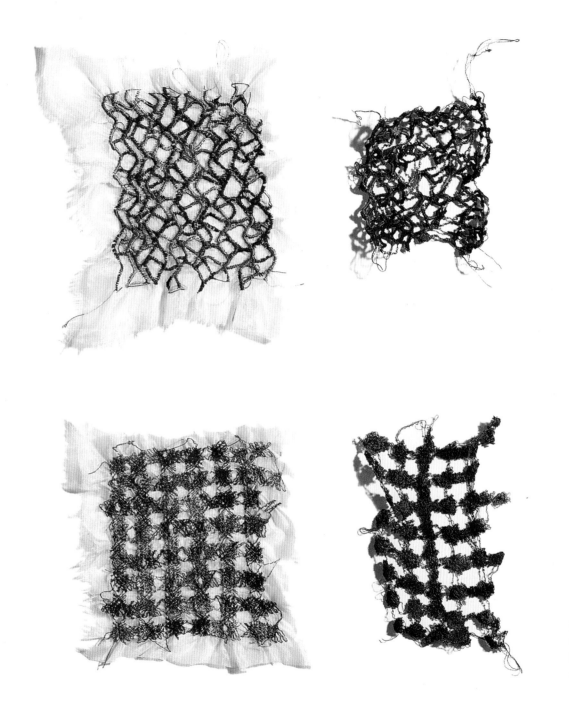

Patterns stitched onto
water-soluble fabric which
is dissolved away leaving
only the distorted stitching.

of my Teflon Foot is that it will only allow patterns up to 4mm (⅛in) wide to be stitched, but you can now get wider ones. (Many machines however will deal with this technique effectively using the Satin Stitch Foot.) When the embroidery is finished, hold it under a cold tap, rubbing it between your fingers until all the 'slime' has dissolved, or leave a little if you want to stiffen the fabric slightly.

MACHINE SETTINGS

Set the tension as normal and use the Satin Stitch or Embroidery Foot with the feed dog up.

Chapter 4

Threads & Patterns

Begin to look for new applications:

threads can be stitched together to make braids,

which in their turn can be stitched or woven

together to make a new fabric.

MACHINE-WRAPPED CORDS

Soft or stiff cords can be made for a variety of purposes. I use them as ties and handles on bags and book covers, belts, decorations on cushions and sewn together to make a firm fabric suitable for making masks, belts or vessels. They can be created by zig-zag stitching over different materials such as string, knitting yarn, embroidery thread, piping cord, raffia, twisted cord, wire, strips of fabric, tights, or plain or stuffed knitting ribbon. You can even use it to stitch on open fabrics such as canvas.

MACHINE SETTINGS

Set your sewing machine to a normal tension if using a coloured thread or a loose top tension and a large needle if using metallic threads. Leave the teeth up. You can use the Braiding Foot with a central hole in the front and a 'tunnel' underneath. Alternatively a Pearls 'n' Piping Foot, or the Knit Edge Foot that you use to sew pieces of knitting together, will control the cord and prevent it from jumping about. If you have a sewing

machine with snap-on feet, just remove the foot and make use of the bottom of the bar to stop the cord jumping too much. You also have the option to use no feet at all, or a Quilting Foot, with the teeth dropped, but this requires more control.

Set the zig-zag to its widest width even if you are covering a narrow yarn. This makes it easier to see the stitching and the stitches will pull in tightly as you move along. Use a stitch length 1–2, changing the length every row so that the stitching does not make too obvious a pattern.

Hold the yarn and the two ends of thread at the back of the needle with your left hand, and hold the yarn you are covering in front of the

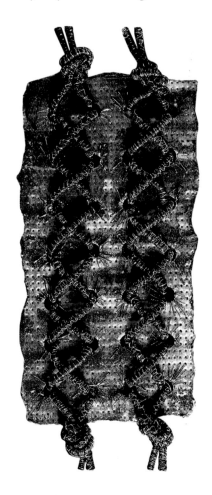

Right: machine-wrapped cords, showing the first row of zig-zag stitching, more rows added to cover the core and another version where the irregular stitching allows the core to bulge out between the stitches.

Far right: machine-wrapped cord stitched through holes punched in painted pelmet vilene.

needle with your right. Start to stitch, keeping a continuous firm tension on the yarn to avoid it being dragged down into the hole in the needle plate, and gently pull it through. Wrap the finished cord around your left hand as it grows and remove it every so often and start again. If you are covering long lengths of yarn, wrap the finished cord around a large bobbin from time to time to control it.

Do not attempt to completely cover the cord in one journey, but do two or three, blending the colours if you are using a variegated thread, or using a different colour for each journey. If the thread breaks, just re-thread the machine and continue, covering the loose ends as you go.

If you would like to add texture you can create lumps or 'beads' by moving the cord back and forth, building up the stitching over a small area. These should be worked on the last journey and can be a different colour to the cord. You can also include small tufts of fabric or threads as you go. Try knotting the cord at intervals. To produce a stiff cord, cover the string or a stiff yarn and make more journeys (Using metallic threads also produces a stiff cord). For a softer cord cover soft knitting wool or strips of tights and make fewer journeys with a coloured thread.

For further decoration you can wrap a cord loosely with a metallic thread, or another machine-wrapped cord. You can zig-zag pre-strung beads on it, knotting both ends together before you stitch to hold them and pushing the beads in place as you sew.

Collection of machine-wrapped cords using different cores and covering threads, coloured and metallic.

STUFFED RIBBON BRAIDS

Knitting ribbon is not so popular for knitting as it used to be but it is still available from some shops, or from general yarn suppliers in larger quantities. It is usually made of rayon which has a lovely gleam, cotton which is very matt, or metallic threads which are more loosely knitted.

Knitting ribbon is ideal for stuffing as it is tubular and you can thread a chunky knitting yarn through it using a long blunt needle. This can be done as an easy job which does not require much attention. The stuffed ribbon can either be smooth, with all the ridges smoothed out, or left unsmoothed which gives an uneven texture. If you would like a finer cord, then use a finer wool or even a slubbed one to give an uneven effect.

Right: the best stitch patterns to use on a stuffed knitting ribbon.

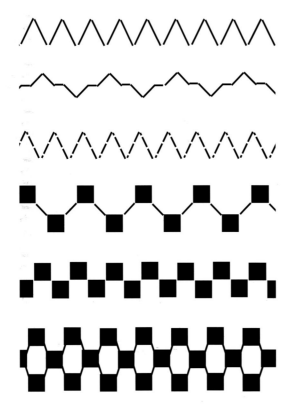

Facing page: collection of stuffed and stitched ribbon braids.

As the knitting ribbon is an open knit, the colour of the stuffing can show through, particularly through the metallic ones. If the chunky wool is black, the colours of the knitting ribbon are denser and more subtle and if it is white then the colours become clearer. If a bright colour chunky wool is used then a glow of that colour shows through the knitting ribbon. When you have stuffed the ribbon, it can be partially covered with zig-zag stitching to give it firmness, or two can be stitched together with automatic patterns which squash them and alter the shape.

MACHINE SETTINGS

Set your machine to a normal tension and stitch length. Attach the Braiding, Knit Edge Foot, or the Pearls 'n' Piping Foot, all with a tunnel underneath which allows the round cord to pass through without being pressed flat. Use a thread in a contrasting colour, or gold which is effective with any coloured knitting ribbon.

Place two cords together and lower the foot. Stitch them with a practical stitch or an automatic pattern. The gathering or elastic stitch which is normally used for stitching butted seams, gives a scalloped effect to the cord. Satin stiches cover more of the cord and flatten it more, but can be useful when joining two sets of cords together to make a fabric. Although the feed dog helps move the cord along while you are stitching, none of feet exert the same pressure as a Standard Foot, so you will have to guide the cord slightly. Because of this many of the patterns look the same as each other, and the multi-directional patterns tend not to work properly.

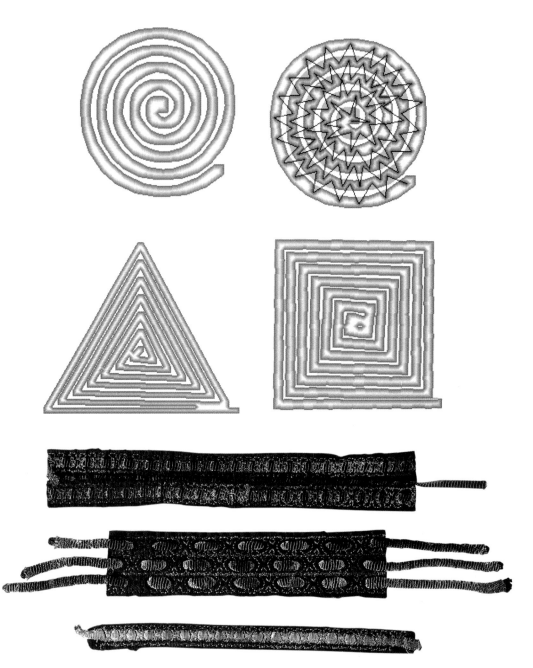

Right (top): a stuffed knitting ribbon spiralled and stitched to make a fabric.

Right (middle): other shapes which could be made in this way.

Right (below): stuffed ribbon braids couched to fabric using automatic patterns, and threaded through eyelet holes in stitched fabric.

STITCHED THREAD BRAIDS

It is perfectly possible to machine stitch without a fabric, and you can make braids by sewing over a number of lengths of yarn, using up all the ones you have had hanging about for years. I find that a mixture of different types

and thicknesses of thread make the best braids, and these can be used as they are, or sewn together to make a complete fabric. Try putting together a 4 ply knitting yarn, a metallic chocolate box type cord, some stranded cotton embroidery thread and a novelty yarn, and stitch them with a darker coloured machine embroidery thread. The colour on the bobbin will show on the completed braid, but does not need to be the same colour as the top thread. Soft yarns and threads make a soft braid while stiffer yarns and metal threads with closer stitching make a stiffer braid.

MACHINE SETTINGS

Use normal tension top and bottom, and leave the teeth up. Either use a Standard Foot or a Cording Foot if you have one, with channels on the top of the foot. Each channel will hold a single thread for a more regular braid. Using the Standard Foot will give a more irregular effect.

FLAT BRAIDS

Sew a few yarns, threads, narrow ribbons or fabric strips together, keeping all the yarns in a bowl, box or carrier bag on the floor. Make sure that they can run freely and knot the ends together to stop them slipping. Place them under the foot and lower the foot to hold them in place. The threads will snake back-and-forth and twist around each other. I would advise letting this happen as it adds interest to the finished braid. Hold the yarns gently at the back of the machine with your left hand and in front of the machine with your right.

MACHINE SETTINGS

Sew the braid with a stretch stitch, or 3 step-zig-zag. Use a short to medium stitch length and the widest width setting for your machine.

ROUND BRAIDS

Sew a number of yarns, threads, narrow ribbons or fabric strips together using either the foot with a tunnel underneath (usually used for joining knitted edges), or the Pearls and Piping Foot. You can do without a foot at all, just making use of the sewing foot holder on some machines to stop the threads leaping about. Keep all the yarns in a bowl, box or carrier bag on the floor as before. Sew the braid with a plain zig-zag stitch set at the widest width, twisting the threads slightly, first clockwise and then anti-clockwise, to give a variegated effect.

MACHINE SETTINGS

Use normal tension top and bottom, and leave the teeth up. Either use a Standard Foot or a Cording Foot if you have one, with channels on the top of the foot. Each channel will hold a single thread for a more regular braid. Using the Standard Foot will give a more irregular effect.

JOINING BRAIDS TOGETHER

Hold the braids even more firmly at the back and the front of the machine to avoid them curving as you sew. If they do curve, pull on one side or the other to straighten them up again. Stitch using the same three step zig-zag, or a fagotting stitch, for joining flat braids.

DISTORTION AND CURVES

If you pull one braid gently as you join two together, the braid will curve to that side. Then while adding a new braid to the inner curve, pull again to curve even more. The more rows you add and the harder you pull, the more it will curve. If you join two inner curves together and then the outer curves together alternately you will get a chevron 'pleated' fabric.

Next spread (left): collection of stitched thread braids using a variety of thick and thin embroidery threads, stitched with three step zig-zag.

Next spread (right): fabrics made by stitching a number of stitched thread braids together.

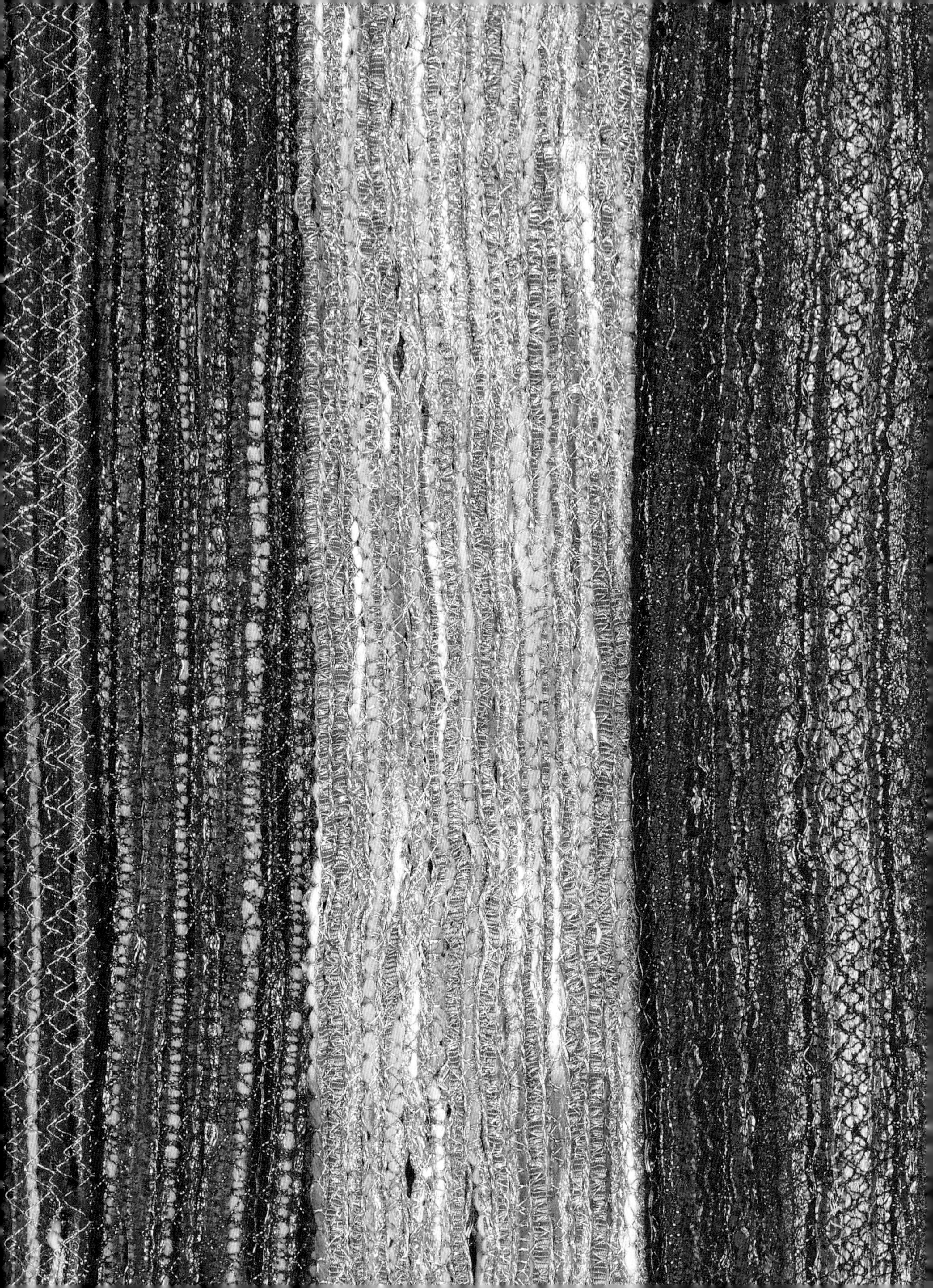

STITCHED PATTERN BRAIDS

Rows of satin stitch embroidery patterns on a non-fraying fabric can be built up in layers to make the most wonderful rich braids which can be used to decorate almost anything. The practical stitches and open patterns are not strong enough unless you use them to couch a narrow ribbon as a base to build up on. If you use felt to stitch on, you can cut the patterns out and use them as they are, or apply them onto more stitching to build up the pattern. If they are only stitched down at intervals, you can thread machine wrapped cords through them, or raise up sections of them with tiny rolls of felt or cylindrical beads. You can also stitch on the bias of a firm fabric so that it does not fray when you cut it. The stitching can be worked in straight lines or in curves, but draw the required curve on the fabric using a dressmaker's pencil to guide you.

MACHINE SETTINGS

Use the Satin Stitch or Embroidery Foot, keep the feed dog up, and use normal tensions on the bottom and a slightly looser tension on the top as this gives the best looking satin stitch.

Find a piece of felt and stitch two rows of something like long and short stitch, or a herringbone pattern next to each other as a base. Then along the side of this, about 2½cm (1in) away, stitch a row of satin stitch ovals. Cut this second strip out and lay it on top of the first stitching. See whether it looks better flat or whether you can 'hoop' it, twist it, or twist two strips together. When you are satisfied with the result, secure the cut strip to the base with a series of thin bars of satin stitch.

You can also stitch braids on water-soluble fabric, but I stitch two or three lines of straight stitching first so that the whole thing does not fall to pieces, and then stitch overlapping rows of patterns over the top. When the fabric is dissolved, you are left with a stitched braid without any fabric bulk. These dissolved fabric braids can be applied to another design, or on top of a stitched pattern braid (see water-soluble fabrics page 58).

Facing page: rich satin stitch patterns ready for cutting into strips.

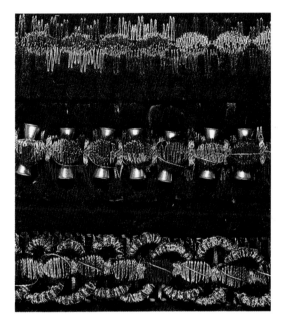

Left: the finished braids, piled up in layers, one with machine-wrapped cord threaded through, and humped over gold beads.

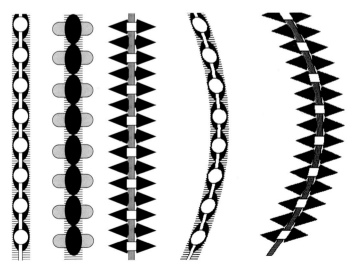

Below: layers of stitched patterns making rich braids.

PLAITS AND BRAIDS

All of the braids and the machine-wrapped cords described previously can be plaited together to make belts or tie-backs for curtains. Once plaited the plaits are stitched together to make a totally new fabric. You can combine some of the methods to mix narrow and wide, round and flat and cords and braids to give a most exciting result. Also just plaiting the stitched thread braids together and then sewing them to each other gives a soft, flexible fabric that can be used to make cushions, or parts of jackets.

PLAITS

Either three- or four-strand plaits are effective, but there are two ways to do this which give quite different results. If you fold a flat braid as you plait it, folding each strand towards the centre as you plait, you will get a firm plait. If you keep it flat as you plait, you will see the stitching and texture of the braids better, and the plait will be looser and more interesting. With a round cord it does not matter which method you use.

MACHINE SETTINGS

To stitch the plaits together, use the 3-step zig-zag, or straight stitch, as it will be more-or-less invisible. Hold two plaits together and stitch them, add another plait and stitch it to the first pair, and continue like this. Be careful that you do not let the piece curve as you stitch.

Right (top): method of making a three-strand plait: right strand over the middle one, then the left hand strand over the middle one. Pull tight.

Right (bottom): method of making a four-strand plait - take the right hand strand under the one to its left and over the next strand. Take the left hand strand over the one to its right.

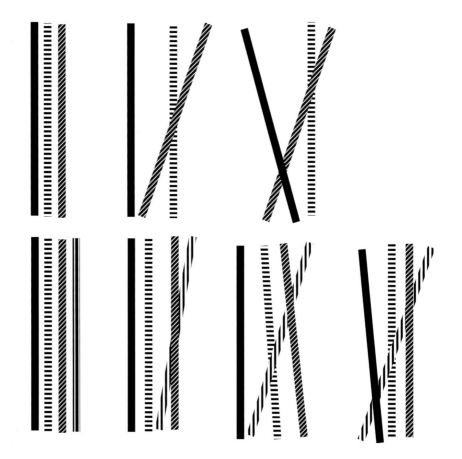

Left: fabric made by
stitching plaited stitched
thread braids together.

Next spread (left): three-
and-four strand plaits
made using the previous
methods of making braids.

Next spread (right): fabric
made by stitching plaited
stitched thread braids
together.

WOVEN PATTERNS

Any strips of fabric with patterns stitched on them, machine-wrapped cords, or any of the braids previously described, can be woven together to make a new fabric which is rich, flexible and has plenty of body without being too heavy.

Cutting the strips with rotary cutters makes short work of the job, and you can then pin one set of strips to a cork bathmat or piece of expanded polystyrene, pinning the strips at one end only so that you can weave the other set of strips through them. When all is done, pin through both layers of on weaving the edge, remove the holding pins and stitch the whole thing together using running stitch. This should go right round the outside, but also across the centre two or three times in each direction to really secure it. The raw edges can be covered by sewing more strips of fabric, or wide velvet ribbon, on to each edge.

USING ROTARY CUTTERS

These cutters make short work of cutting strips for weaving, whether strips of decorated fabrics, or between rows of patterns stitched in long lines. A rotary cutter is a wheel-shaped blade on a handle with a guard which you must remove before use. Properly used, these cutters cut a really smooth line along the length and are much faster than scissors.

There are a number of makes of rotary cutters which are all effective, but I prefer the largest size of 6cm (2⅜in) If you cannot find these then use the 4½cm (1¾in) cutters. To cut a strip, place the fabric on a cutting mat (which you can buy at an art shop) or a piece of thick card, and press a ruler or other straight edge on to it with one hand. Run the cutter down the edge of the ruler with the other hand, keeping the blade straight up and down. The cutting edge is razor sharp at first and the blade can be sharpened or replaced when it becomes blunter. When you have practised using these cutters, try cutting squares, triangles and diamonds with them and then curved shapes. You can look down at the blade and guide it smoothly around the curve.

When you have finished using them, replace the guard to protect both the blade and yourself. Separate blades can be bought which will cut chevrons, as pinking shears do, but in a smooth pattern without nicks, or blades that will cut wavy or wiggly lines. Cutting strips with these and then stitching them with a pattern that gives similar wavy lines adds emphasis, and it looks less rigid than a straight line.

Left (top): woven strips of
patterned stitching and
metallic and velvet ribbons.

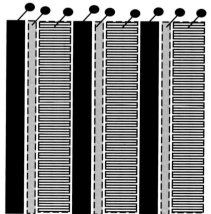

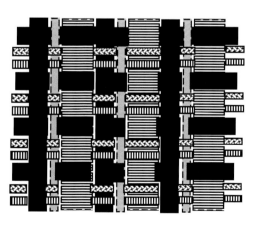

Far left: strips of stitched
fabrics and stitched thread
braids pinned to a board.

Near left: more strips
woven through them to
make a fabric.

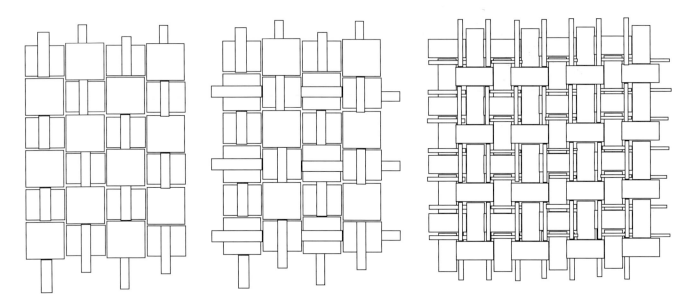

Above: different woven
patterns using thick and
thin braids and stitched
strips.

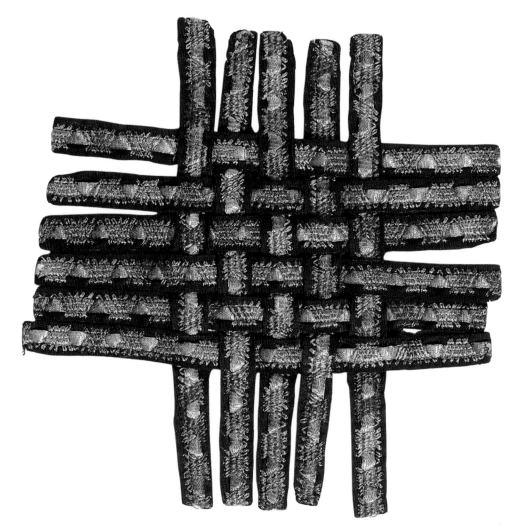

Right: woven strips of
stuffed ribbon braids
applied to strips of felt
with a stitched pattern.

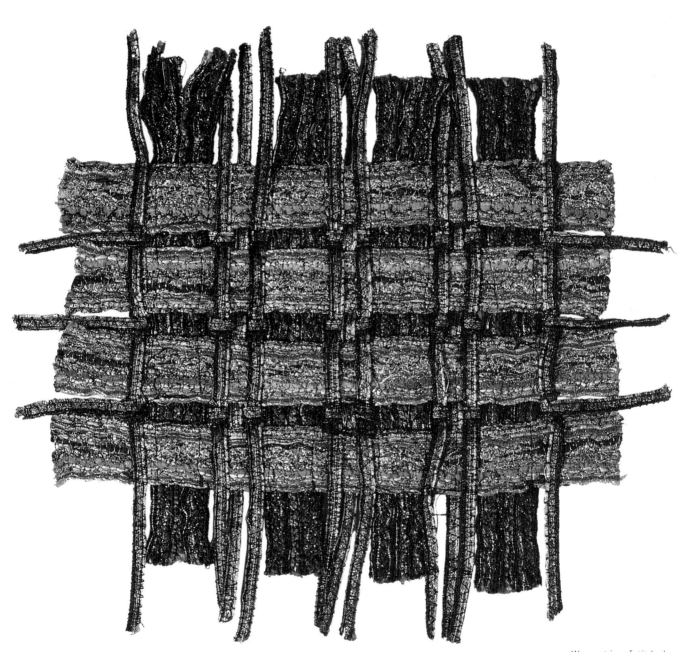

Woven strips of stitched
threads braids of different
widths.

Chapter 5

Larger Patterns

Apply the new technologies:

the larger patterns are much more exciting to play

with and can be adapted to make them more

individual. The final joy is being able to scan and

stitch your own larger motifs.

USING LARGER PATTERNS TO DECORATE FABRICS

Facing page: layers of organza and felt decorated with sections of a leaf pattern, moving diagonally over the fabric between every section. The fabrics were cut away from the back after some of the stitching and a flower pattern in multi-coloured thread stitched on top, again moving diagonally over the fabric between sections.

If you have a machine with a sideways motion you will be able to stitch larger patterns in continuous rows or as a spot pattern all over the fabric. You can move each either horizontally, vertically or diagonally between each repeat. This can either be done freehand, or the sequence can be programmed into your machine and repeated endlessly.

These larger patterns are usually much less rigid than the narrower patterns. They are often floral or pictorial and many of them are quite classic. Some of them are intended for use as edgings, such as chevrons or scallops, but these can be just as useful as the all-over patterns. Some of the patterns are in running stitch, some in triple running satin, some in satin stitch, and some are use a combination of these stitches. Stitching all over a fabric, or layers of fabric with these patterns gives a freer effect than when using the narrow patterns, and I am particularly fond of them built up in layers in different directions.

MACHINE SETTINGS

It is sometimes difficult to stitch these patterns in straight rows, as the fabric moves about in different directions as it stitches, and you cannot use the edge as a guide, so if you can alter the pressure on the Presser Foot, set it to the maximum. Use the Satin Stitch Foot and normal tensions and leave the teeth up.

You will need a stabiliser of some sort, but even so you might find that the pattern goes off at an angle. Make a feature of this and do overlapping rows that are not supposed to be perfect which give added richness as well as hiding any mistakes. If you are stitching over scraps of fabric of different weights, or applied pieces of felt or previously worked stitching which are quite thick, you will find it almost impossible to produce an accurate pattern. You could try laying a sheet of cold water-soluble fabric over the whole thing, but I found it better to do short lengths of the pattern all over the place (or even individual motifs), rather than to try for perfection.

Right: using a built-in larger (continuous) pattern in bands all in the same direction.

Far right: using a built-in larger (continuous) pattern in bands, each row in a different direction.

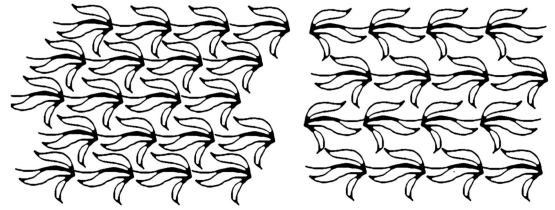

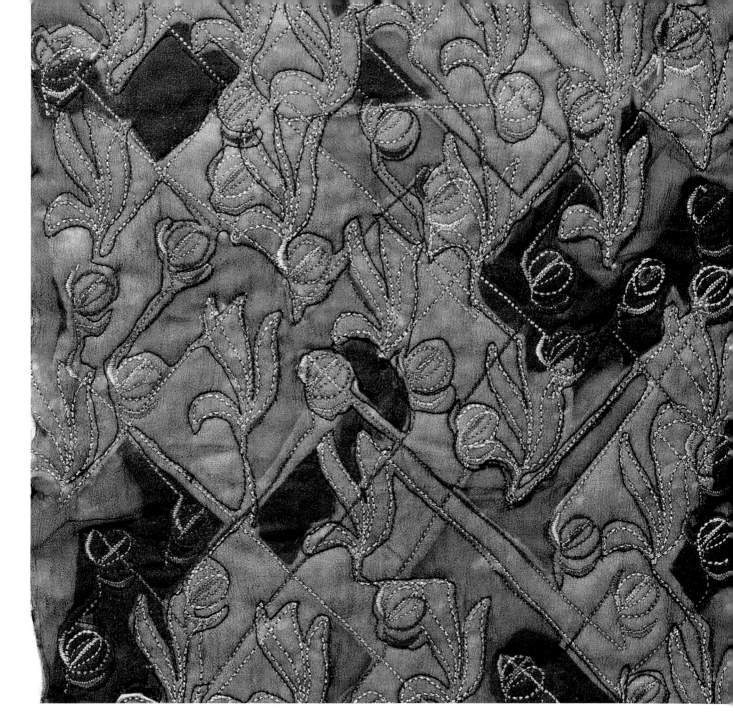

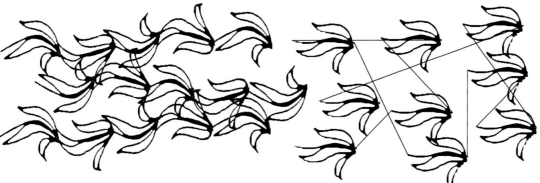

Far left: using a built-in larger (continuous) pattern by swinging the fabric as the pattern is stitched for a less formal effect.

Left: using a built-in larger (continuous) pattern by travelling in different directions before each motif is sewn separately.

Above: an edging pattern used irregularly and in different widths to secure scraps of coloured silk.

Far right: scraps of fabrics secured with a stretch stitch, cut and restitched twice in each direction.

PRODUCING A MIRROR IMAGE OF A PATTERN

This feature flips a stitch or segment of a pattern. Some machines only flip it horizontally, and others will also flip it vertically. This facility allows you to build up borders and make wider patterns which have more scope. This feature, along with the change of direction between each segment and the combining of two or more segments from different patterns, gives a more individual result. You will have to look in your manual for instructions on storing your own patterns in the memory, as each machine has a slightly different method.

CHANGING THE STITCHING

Satin stitch patterns are supposed to be worked with a slightly looser top tension to give the best effect, so check this on a small sample first. You could loosen the bobbin tension and tighten the top tension so that the underneath thread comes up and gives a different coloured edging to the satin stitch. Or you could leave the bobbin thread as it is, the top thread tension slightly loose and work upside-down. Sometimes the top layer of stitching sinks into the background (visually) and does not show enough, so a very dark coloured edging would define the pattern well. Another way of doing this is to work an outline of narrow satin stitch in black or any dark colour around the pattern, or along one edge of it. This will have to be done freehand, but you will not need to put the work in a frame as the layers of fabric will give you enough body to hold it as you stitch.

INDIVIDUAL LARGE MOTIFS

The facility for stitching separate motifs or segments of a large pattern is invaluable. They can be used as a spot pattern over a whole area, overlapping to build up richness, or cut out and used as 'slips' applied to other stitching. The motifs can be flipped horizontally, and often vertically, to make more complex patterns, and this can be programmed into your machine and repeated (see your own manual for instructions for your model).

Try stitching the pattern with a loose top tension, with different coloured threads in the bobbin and through the needle, and also working upside down, which gives a two-coloured effect on the back, and usually a nice texture as well. Two threads through the needle do not usually work at all well here, as the pattern clogs up, but you could try a shiny thread on a fabric of nearly the same colour, or close colours such as navy-blue on black velvet, or white on white and then paint it afterwards.

EMBROIDERY ATTACHMENT

Many of the top machines now have an embroidery attachment which allows even larger motifs to be stitched extremely accurately. This attachment slides onto your machine and requires a special embroidery frame which is firmly attached to it. You can only use the Darning Foot (sometimes a special one comes with the attachment) and the feed dog is left up. Having set the machine up, you push a 'start' button and walk away, leaving the machine to get on with the stitching. It is wonderful – just like having an assistant in your work room, leaving you to get on with another job!

Right: typical large motifs built in to a sewing machine.

Facing page: some of the individual motifs stitched using the embroidery attachments or beds, which are either built in to the machine or come on extra cards.

Many of these motifs, which come on a separate card that slides into a slot at the side of the sewing machine, are designed to be worked in more than one colour. The first section is stitched and then the machine stops, telling you to change to another thread. You do not have to do this and the whole thing can be worked in one colour, or using a variegated thread. With some machines you can specify how many colours you can use for each motif, either two or three, or all in one colour. You can stitch just half the motif, for example, just the leaves of an ear of corn, or one section of a more geometric pattern. Then repeat this section by skipping the others, pushing a button to move along to the section you want.

CHANGING THE SETTINGS

Again the motif, or parts of it, can be flipped, mirrored or rotated, according to which machine you are using. Take advantage of this by flipping or rotating the different parts of the pattern while you are working.

DANGLES

Small dangles, or tassels can be stitched to the end of a cord, or hung from an embroidery as further decoration. These can be made by cutting out two pieces of the same stitched shape and one should be mirrored by placing them back-to-back (as long as it is not a symmetrical shape), stitching around most of the shape by hand and then filling the hollow with shredded polyester wadding.

If you cut out two shapes, such as a large V, stitch the inside edges of each V to make it a hollow shape, and then stitch them together on the outside, stuffing as you go. You will produce a shape that looks rather like a seed pod, and a number of them will make wonderful dangles that can echo similar shapes stitched on the embroidery.

Right: putting three different sizes of the same star pattern together: the star large and small, a medium size star worked on top of a large star, and the three sizes worked on top of each other.

Above: patterns that can be made using the star in three different sizes and colours. If stitched on felt, the stars can be cut out and laid on a background on top of, or overlapping, each other. Holes can be cut in them, fabrics placed underneath, or they can be folded to make raised patterns.

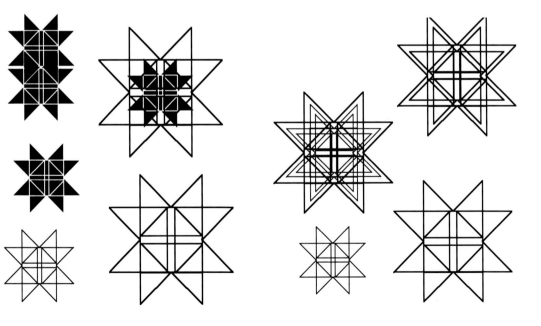

90

PUTTING DIFFERENT SIZES TOGETHER

Some machines allow you to change the size of the large patterns, whether it is one of the built-in ones or on a separate card. This is immensely useful for designing and removes any absolute regularity when the motif is repeated. You can work with three different sizes inside each other, the first one in the largest size, the second slightly smaller, and the third one smaller still. This can be varied by rotating the image each time it is stitched. If you do this to a teddy bear with a bow round its neck, the result will be most peculiar, but try it with one of the abstract patterns and something really exciting emerges. These variations can be put into the memory so you do not have to keep changing the settings (see your manual for details).

MACHINE SETTINGS

Machines have various methods of changing the size of a motif, so you will need to check this in your manual. Leave the tensions normal, use the recommended foot and leave the teeth up.

Try stitching rows of the same, simple motif in different sizes and on top of each other to make a rich border. (Who said machine embroidery was quicker than hand embroidery?) If you stitch three different sizes of the star motif in the diagrams and cut them out, you can place one on top of another one slightly larger with the layers stitched together. If the stars are stitched on felt, then you can cut holes in one of them before you lay it over another. Further hand or machine embroidery will enhance the design. Geometric shapes such as these stars can be folded, the points folded to the centre or the whole star folded assymetrically.

Either one set of points, or two opposing points, can be folded in.

With leaf and flower patterns you can create a much more realistic garden effect by putting different sizes together, as well as using the mirror imaging and rotating facility. Work all these in a mass in different sizes, starting with the leaves and then adding the flowers – some with tall stems and some with shorter ones.

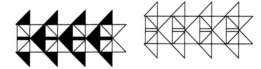

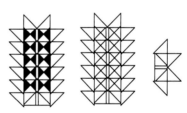

Left (top): stitched stars, using three different sizes were decorated with hand embroidery. Small ones were cut out and applied to larger ones, and some with holes cut in them were backed with another fabric.

Left (bottom): holes cut in the spaces of the large stars, which are then laid over a patterned fabric.

ADDING FURTHER EMBROIDERY

The Elizabethans used a technique of working separate flower motifs, usually in canvas work, which were afterwards applied to another fabric. These were called 'slips'. In ecclesiastical embroidery, many motifs were worked separately and applied to another fabric with further stitching added. This method was also used in China, with such a fine silk fabric that it is hard to tell that it was applied rather than being stitched straight onto the ground. This method is extremely flexible, and the large motifs on modern sewing machines can also be adapted for use in this manner. Stitch them first and then cut out and apply them. You can move the motifs about to get the best result, and if one turns out not to be so perfectly stitched you can discard it, or cut it up and use parts of it.

Some machine motifs are stitched quite densely with all or parts of them in satin stitch, and some are more openly stitched, often using triple straight stitch to give a more definite line. With the densely stitched ones you will probably need to secure them to another fabric with a straight stitch, and can then outline them with narrow satin stitch to give more definition. If you stitch them on felt, this outlining will make them seem slightly padded, or you could alternatively pad them with a smaller shape cut from felt.

It is then up to you to decide whether you add more embroidery to the ground fabric or not, and here you can use the tiny sections of some of the satin stitch patterns to build up texture, or outline the motif with rows of straight stitch. With the more openly stitched motifs you can bond them onto a ground fabric, and then stitch all over them to secure them firmly, add interest, and improve the handle of the fabric by giving it more body. Some motifs are just outlined with narrow satin stitch, and I like to cut them out, place them on a decorated fabric, and fill the spaces with very fine granite stitch, or massed free running, to fill the empty spaces. Leaving the satin stitched edges unstitched causes them to rise up a little from the background.

Right: an automatic flower pattern stitched on muslin and cut out and applied to a decorated fabric. The empty spaces were filled in with granite stitch worked with the foot off and dropped teeth.

Facing page (below): one of the large motifs built into a machine was stitched and traced on to paper. This was used as a pattern to cut out in painted fabrics, bonded onto a backing fabric, and curved lines of running stitch worked all over the surface to secure them and add movement.

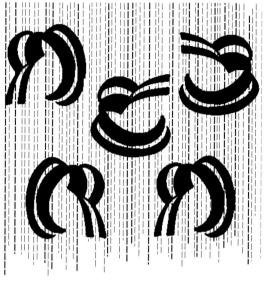

Far left (top): a large pattern stitched individually at different angles, can be covered with straight lines of stitching to blend the colours and give the fabric body.

Left (top): lines of stitching at different angles, or in shallow curves, can add movement and excitement to the design.

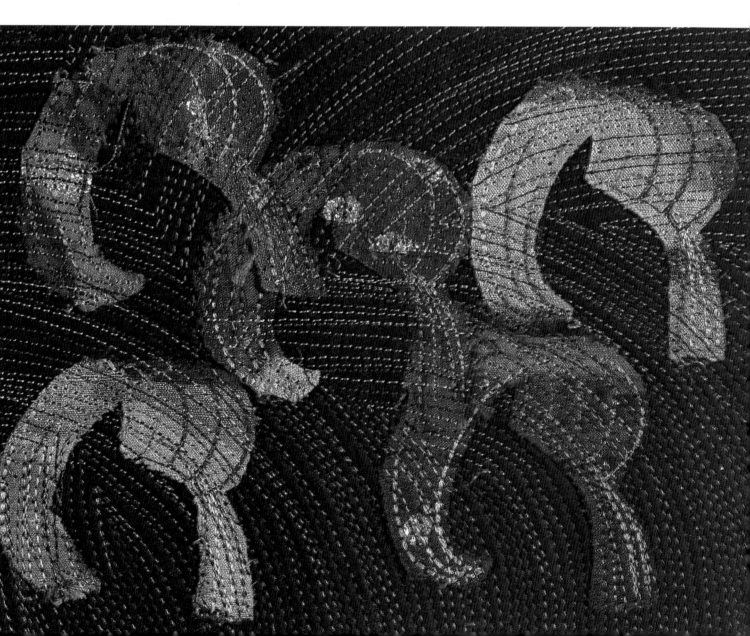

COMBINING PATTERNS

To give a more individual look to your work and to make it richer and more exciting, you can build up layers of stitching on top of each other by combining different patterns. Two or even three large patterns can be used together, or a narrow pattern over a large one, or a large pattern over a narrow one. The essential ingredient is to use contrasting coloured thread so that the patterns do not merge into each other. The stitching can be worked in straight rows, or the fabric swung from side to side as you stitch (see swinging stitches on page 00).

Cover a background fabric with either strips or squares of different fabrics, or a single piece of painted, printed or sprayed fabric, and then cover the whole thing with rows of a large pattern (preferably one of the linear ones). You can either keep them all going in the same direction or back and forth in two directions which has the added advantage of avoiding any ruckles in the fabric which might appear if you only stitch in

one direction. Then give the fabric a quarter turn, change the thread to something that contrasts with the first coloured thread and the fabric, perhaps gold or a very dark colour and stitch another pattern in rows at right angles to the first. It is best to choose a satin stitch pattern for this second layer so that it shows up, but it could be a narrow or a wide pattern.

When using the embroidery for mounting on a book cover, then back the first layer with felt or pelmet vilene and put another layer of felt underneath before you stitch the second layer. Keep the bobbin thread the same colour as the backing fabric so that you will not have to line the finished embroidery.

The layers of fabric and stitching. It looks rich, interesting and exciting because of the multiple layers of pattern. It also gives you a chance to make your embroidery quite individual, even in comparision work produced with the same machine and the same patterns.

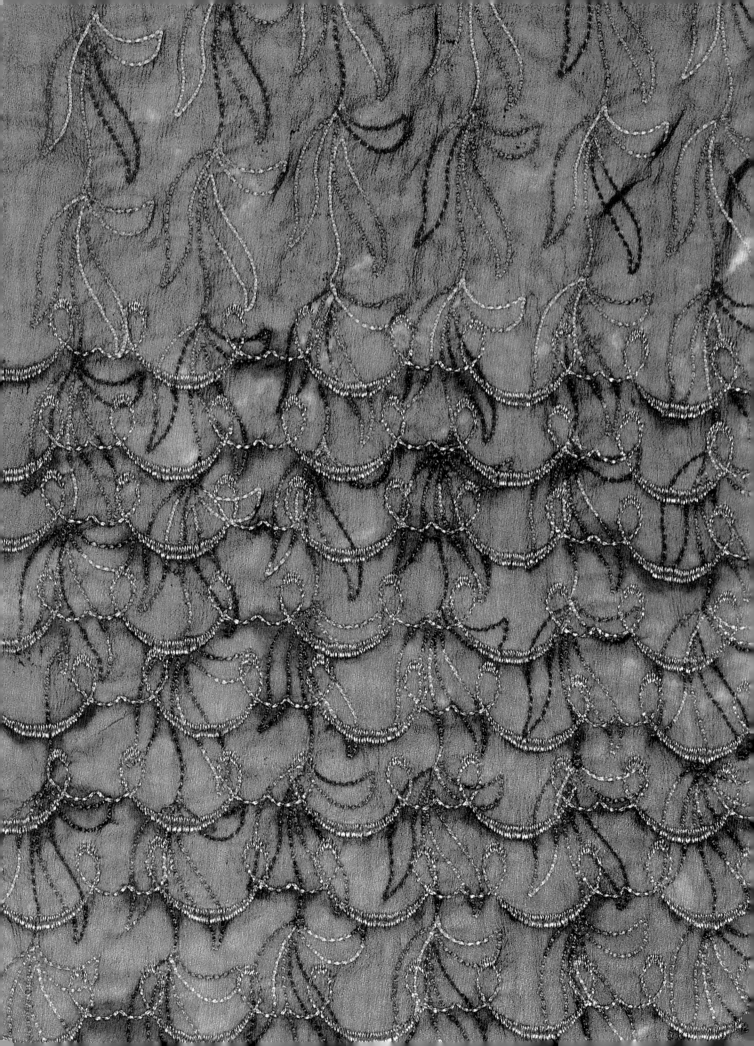

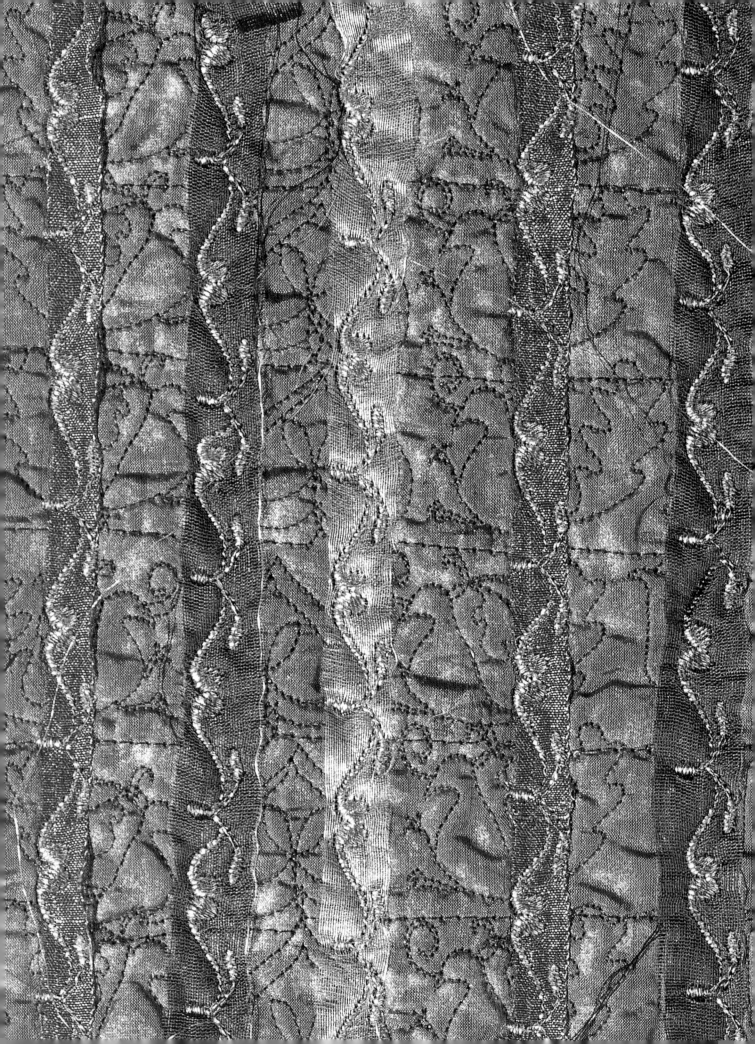

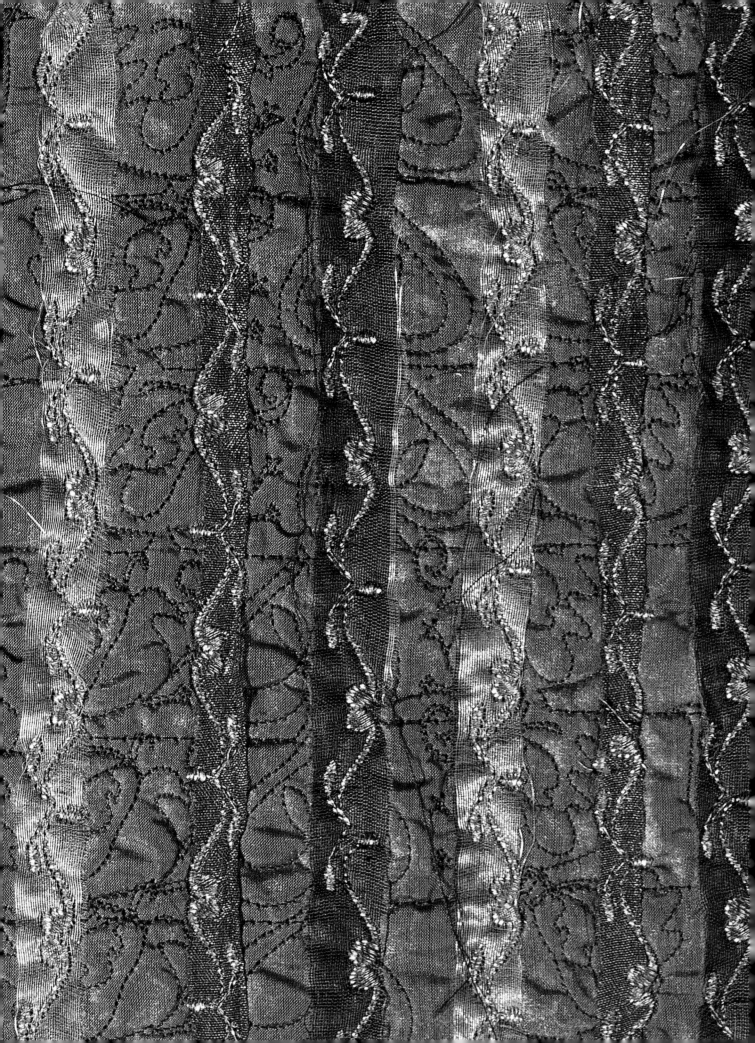

Chapter 6

Scanned Patterns

Apply the new technologies:

some machines have a scanning attachment, which

is much the easiest way to stitch your own

drawings or designs, any number of times.

SCANNED IMAGES

A few sewing machines have an optional scanning attachment. This is powered separately, and includes a small black-and-white hand scanner and a memory card on which you can save your scanned images. The card fits into the same slot in the machine as the commercial memory cards, but you must ensure that you buy the correct one as each make of machine uses a different scanner and memory card.

CHOOSING SPECIFICATIONS

Scanned images are quick and easy to use and enable the production of a variety of effects. First of all you switch on the main part of the scanner and choose which type of stitching you wish to use and the direction of the stitches, pressing the relevant buttons. You could choose a line stitch, satin stitch (or cross stitch on the Janome machines) or the weaving or Tatami stitch which can be worked in different directions. You then choose what size the image is to be. It can be stitched either the same size as the original, or smaller. The scan can also be mirrored or rotated and moved up, down or sideways. All this information is saved for you in the main part of the scanning

attachment. The largest size of the final stitched image varies from machine to machine and is from about 9cm (3½in) square to a 9 x 11½cm (3½ x 4½in) rectangle.

SCANNING

Lay the drawing to be scanned in the lid of the scanner which has a clip to hold it. Press the button on the movable scanner head to start it and holding the button down on the

scanning head so that the light stays on, draw the head slowly over your drawing. If you go too fast, the scanner will tell you and you will have to start again from the beginning. The image appears on a small screen on the main body of the scanning machine and you can see from here whether it is straight or not, or whether it is the right section and in the right place. Then you follow the instructions for memorizing the scan, remove the memory card from the scanner and slot it into the machine. You must follow your instruction manual exactly for the whole procedure, but once you have done one or two, you will find the process an extremely simple one.

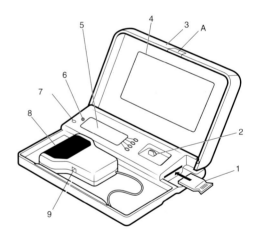

DIFFERENT COLOURS

Most scanners allow you to scan separate parts of a design using different coloured threads, usually two or three, although you can use more. You need to draw the design very carefully for this, and decide which way up the design should be. Commercial patterns will often have detailed information such as a blue bow around a teddy

Right: key for scanner
1 Memory card for Scan 'n Sew 11
2 Power switch/Eject button
3 Cover (Press 'A' to open)
4 Reference chart
5 Display screen
6 Receptacle for AC adaptor
7 Display adjustment dial
8 Scanner
9 Scanner ON/OFF button

bear's neck which needs very exact drawing, but if you think of the different layers of colour in a freer way it is much easier. Try a line drawing over solid shapes and work the line in a narrow satin stitch.

DISTORTED SCANS

Normally you pull the scanner straight over your drawing. You can also experiment by curving it as you scan, or wiggling it, or lifting it up in the air every inch or so or changing direction. As long as your thumb remains on the button it will continue scanning. Gentle distortion will give you a number of leaf shapes from just the original one, or give excitement and movement to a drawing that is a bit stiff.

CHOOSING YOUR SCANNER

I have tried all the scanners on the market, and they are more-or-less the same as each other and all easy-to-use. However this area of technology changes rapidly and the ones I am now familiar with may all be out-of-date by the time you are reading this, so explore what is available. Either buy a scanner that fits onto your present machine, as the Janome scanner does or buy a separate machine and scanner such as the Bernette Deco and keep your present sewing machine. The Pfaff uses a slightly different system from which you can scan in to your computer and then digitize the scan for sewing using the Pfaff software. This is then downloaded onto your sewing machine.

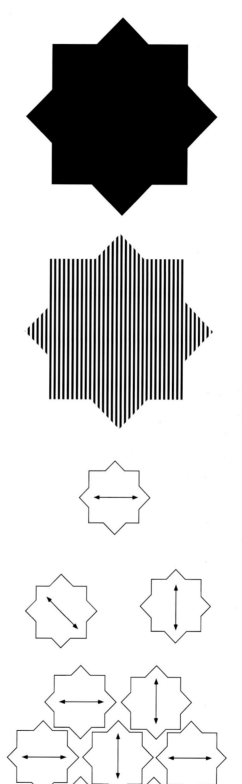

Left (top): these drawings will give different results even if the same stitch is specified on the scanner.

Left (middle): the quatrefoil is scanned in different directions, and the stitching will be different in each one.

Left (bottom): if the stitching is worked in a shiny thread, and the motif placed with the stitching in different directions on the background fabric, there will be a distinct change of tone which will add life to the design. If the motifs are padded before they are applied, the change of tone will be emphasized.

101

DRAWINGS FOR SCANS

If you are using one of your own drawings which has fine or indistinguishable lines, you may need to redraw it with thicker lines or the scanner will not be able to read it. I use a fine black felt pen for this. You can draw smooth or broken lines and fill in some areas as solid black as a contrast. Two pens are included in the scanner package so you can compare the width with your own pens. The lines should not be too close together, or they will not be read as separate lines, but don't be too fussy about this as the results can often be more interesting than you expect. Only use flat surfaces for scanning as problems will occur if you try and scan something that is bumpy or textured, even if it is covered with a piece of plastic.

Illustrations (this page and facing page): images to scan.

WHAT TO SCAN

You can scan photocopies, rubbings, computer printouts, block prints on paper, patterns sprayed through stencils, spattered or marbled papers, printed or woven fabrics, skeletonised leaves, or even previously worked stitching. Dover Books are full of copyright-free images that you can scan parts of and use out of context (see **Further Reading**, page 127). If you want to scan images from other books, magazines, cards or wrapping papers which are not copyright-free, you must get advance permission.

One idea is to scan in a design, stitch it, scan the stitching and stitch it again. The image will change gradually with each stage. Quite surprising areas of complex pattern and textures can be scanned which will look wonderful as all-over backgrounds. If you are trying to scan something that is demanding on the scanner, it will either tell you that it cannot do it, or it will try very hard and the results will be a great surprise. The unexpected and instant results of this technique make it great fun to work with.

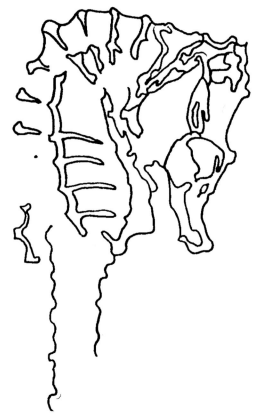

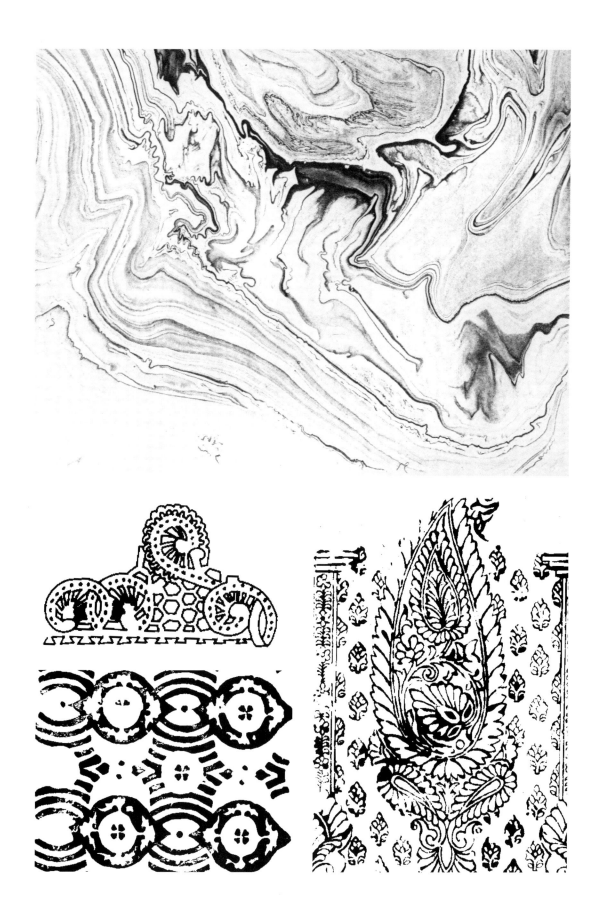

STITCHING THE SCAN

The scanner adapts the image to be stitched, so once the card is slotted into the sewing machine, the bobbin filled and the needle threaded, the machine can stitch your design for you. As you watch it – mesmerized for the first few times – you will see the needle moves from one area to another in a way that you would not have predicted. This leaves loose threads on the surface which you will need to cut away afterwards. If there are too many loose threads on your design, then try scanning it again in another direction to see if there is a difference. A simple, filled in design will leave almost no threads, while one with large areas of 'bitty' texture might have many – but this can also create an attractive effect.

I find that a size 40 machine thread is usually the best to use as a 30 will often be too thick. Any tricky threads can be put onto the bobbin and the work stitched upside-down. The top and bobbin tensions can be changed – I particularly like the effect when the top thread is quite loose, and the bobbin thread a bit tighter than normal, so that you get both threads showing on the back which will then become the top of the embroidery.

You can use any stabiliser you like, and if the reverse of the stitching is to be the right side, then the stabiliser should be used on the top. You can stitch on most fabrics, but remember which is to be your right side as you don't want the best stitching to be on the back of the fabric! You can also stitch a scanned image onto water-soluble fabric, but you should stitch a grid first. Doing the grid is so tedious that I scan in a drawing of a grid and let the machine do all the donkey work for me.

You can decide to use the Tatami (or weaving) stitch. This looks like diagonal rows of very even, solid stitching. The stitching can go in different directions, and you can take advantage of this and the play of light on a shiny thread, by stitching the same motif several times in different directions and using them together on the same piece.

You can also choose the outline stitch which is extremely useful for appliqué, or when you wish to add further free machine embroidery. The outline can be a single line, or either of two widths of satin stitch. On one machine there is also a cross stitch option which gives a lovely, although very regular, texture which looks better on the back. Use the special Darning Foot supplied with the embroidery bed and attach the bed by following the instructions.

MACHINE SETTINGS

Leave the tensions normal, or use a slightly loose top tension which will give the most wonderful results on the back of the fabric, especially if the two threads are different colours. I nearly always work like this now, and turn the embroidery over before I use it on the finished piece. Most machines will not tolerate two threads in the needle when you stitch these patterns, but you can try two fine threads in the bobbin.

You must frame the fabric in the special frame supplied with the machine and attach it according to the instructions. It is quite difficult to place the image accurately, although each manufacturer will give individual instructions. To overcome this I

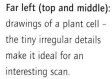

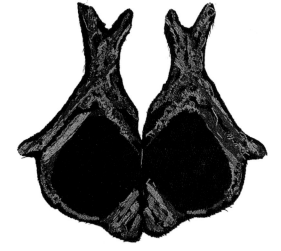

Far left (top and middle): drawings of a plant cell – the tiny irregular details make it ideal for an interesting scan.

Left (top, middle and bottom): scanned drawings of a plant cell which were then stitched onto calico and black felt using a variegated thread.

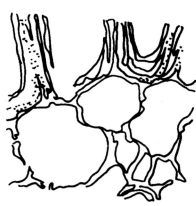

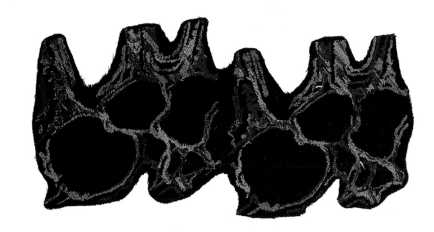

tend to stitch a number of images separately, knowing that I will cut each one out individually and place them on another piece of fabric ready for further stitching. This has the advantage of your being able to use both fronts and backs together and to overlap them if you wish. You do not even have to keep your foot on the pedal as there is a start button on the machine which you press, or on one machine you start with the foot pedal and then it continues by itself. Once you have stitched a number of small pieces, or areas of texture, then it is time to think how you want to use them.

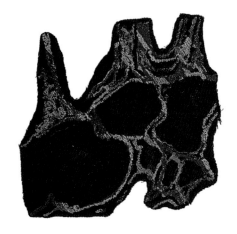

Next spread (left): some stitched motifs previously scanned from drawings.

Next spread (right): an automatic motif was stitched over applied scraps of shot silk. The motif was traced onto paper and scanned, specifying Tatami stitch. The cut-out stitched motifs were applied on top and secured with free running stitch.

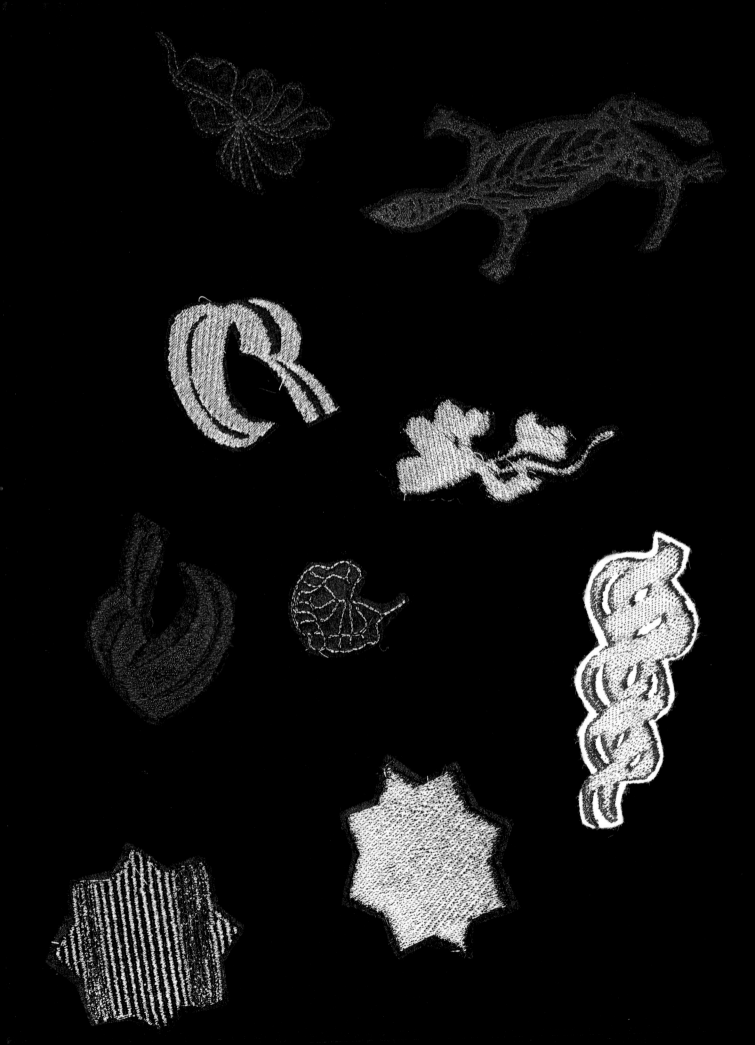

Right (top): my name, designed on the computer and mirrored and doubled. It was printed out so it could then be scanned.

Far right (top): three different parts of the design, each one scanned in separately so that they could be stitched in three different colours.

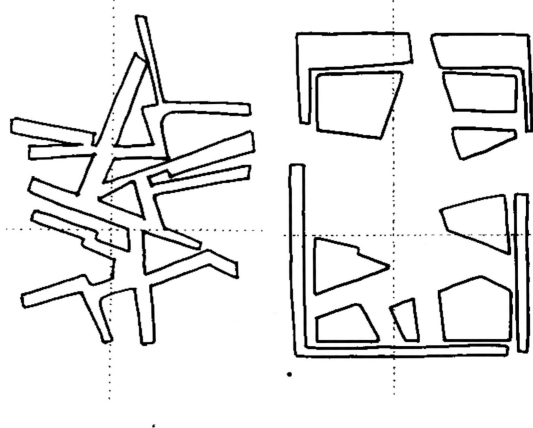

Right (bottom): the complete design, showing how the different parts fit together.

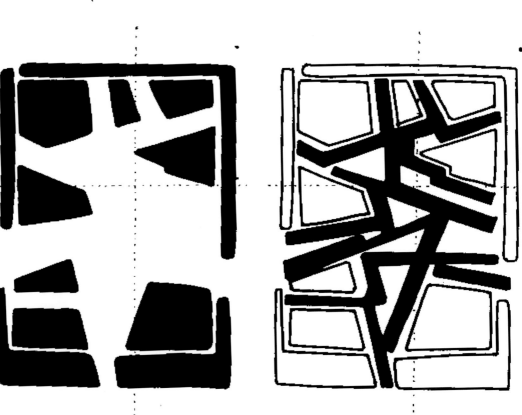

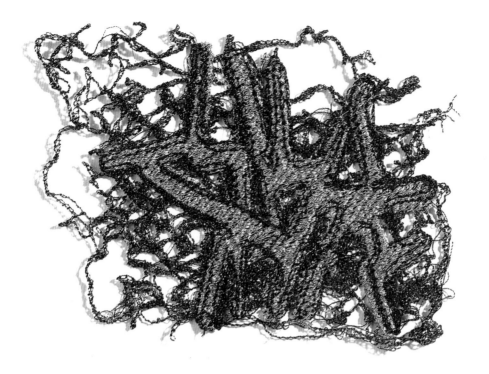

Left (top): the complete design stitched on watersoluble fabric.

Left (bottom): the complete design stitched on to felt using a different colour for each layer.

DEVELOPING THE STITCHING

There are two main ways of using the stitched motif or area of texture. One is to totally cover a background fabric with the stitching, moving the fabric in the frame so that the fabric is mostly covered. This is quite difficult to judge at first but does get easier with practice. Or you can space the stitching out so that more of the background shows and you are making a spot pattern or a border. The other way is to stitch each motif or area of texture separately and cut them out afterwards and place them on another fabric. Both methods have their uses, but I tend to favour the second one as I find it more flexible.

The motifs need to be stitched down, which you can do by hand or using free running stitch, but you will probably feel that you need to add more decoration, probably more hand or machine embroidery. This can be in the form of outlines round the slips, connecting them together and building them into a design. Or it can be that you stitch all over the top of them, blending them into the background fabric and securing them at the same time. You might consider building up the background with stitchery. This is exactly the same problem that arose with the larger patterns except that you have more control over the pieces that you have stitched and have an idea in mind before you started.

Do remember to look at the back of the work as it is so often far more interesting that the front. You can also use both together in one design. Try working on unusual background fabrics such as a very open scrim whch will distort as it is stitched. If this does not work on your machine, back the scrim with calico to keep it firmer. A fabric which always looks beautiful when fairly densely stitched is velvet, so if you are going to use the back of the stitching, put the velvet in the frame upside-down.

EXPERIMENTS

Usually you will need to cut the long threads that are left on the surface when the needle travels to different parts of the pattern, but you could leave them for added interest and couch them down by hand to secure them if you feel they need it. Think of experimenting with additional techniques, such as painting the stitching when you have finished. Work the stitching in shiny white thread on a matt fabric, and then paint it with silk paints or general-purpose fabrics. The paint can be thin and flooded on, allowing it to flow in unexpected directions, or if thicker it can be applied with a flat brush just scraped across the surface of the stitching, hardly touching the background.

Another idea is to try cutting and slashing the stitching to give texture – this is particularly good with the 5mm ($\frac{1}{4}$in) satin stitching, which must have iron-on-vilene firmly attached to the back of the stitching, or a layer of PVA glue, to stop the threads falling out when you cut them.

You could also try stitching some motifs on a fabric, adding some cut-out 'slips' on top of them, and then adding further stitching. Each layer of stitching could be done using a different stitch, for example Tatami for the bottom layer, then a satin stitch outline, and then a fine line pattern.

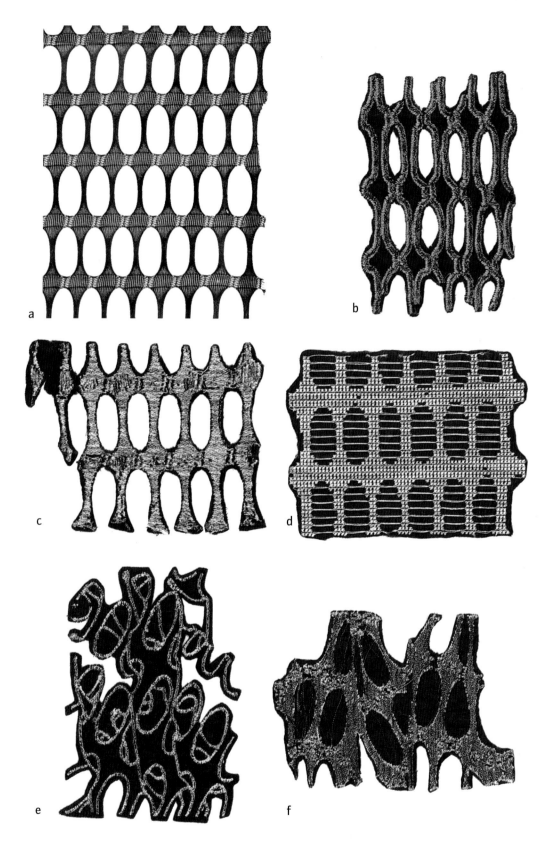

a A photocopy of a piece
   of curtain net was
   scanned and stitched
   using different stitches:
b Satin stitch
c Tatami,or weaving stitch
d Cross stitch
e Scans of an irregularly
   folded piece of net,
   stitched in satin stitch
f Scans of an irregulary
   folded piece of net,
   stitched in Tatami stitch

The scanned net was stitched in a number of different ways and further developed using a number of different methods:

Right and far right (top): stitching from a distorted scan of a drawing of the folded net was outlined with many rows of slip stitching using a loose bobbin tension.

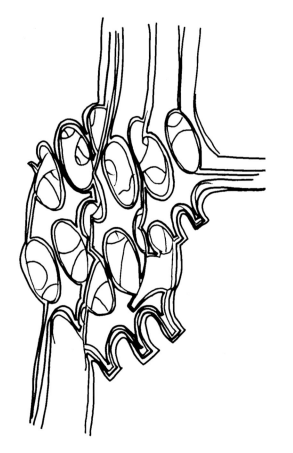
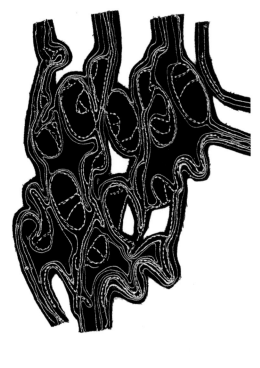

Right (bottom): line and satin stitches. The widest satin stitch was slit with a seam unpicker and covered with white emulsion paint.

Left (bottom): the pattern was stitched using a narrow satin stitch and a cross stitch in layers, with cut strips of satin stitch applied on top.

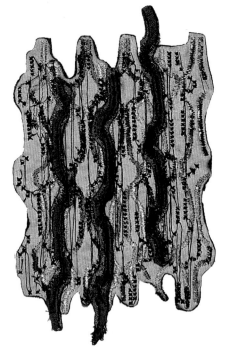
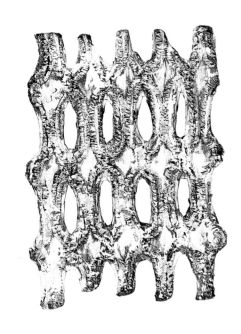

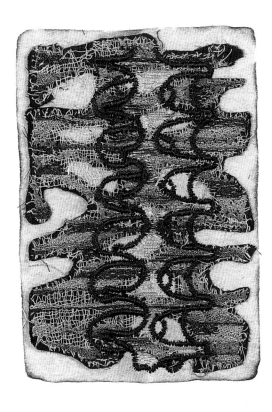

Left: a stitched scan was
worked on black felt, and
shapes cut away from
parts. Muslin was laid over
the top, and more stitching
worked in black using a
scan of a line drawing of a
folded piece of net. Long
stitches were added to fill
in certain areas, worked by
hand using a metallic
thread.

Below: a distorted scan
was stitched onto baked
felt, backed with muslin.
Shapes were cut from
another piece of stitching,
using the same pattern
worked on black, cut out
and applied on top. The
final layer was stitched in
black using a different
scan of a line drawing of a
folded piece of net.

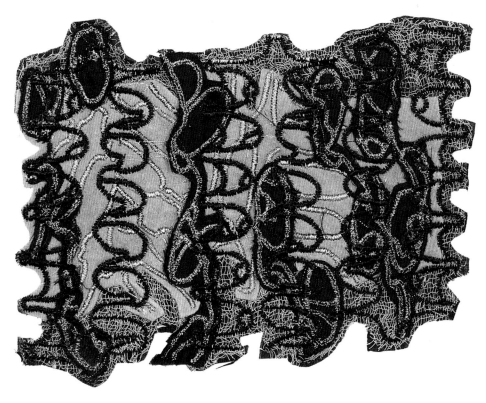

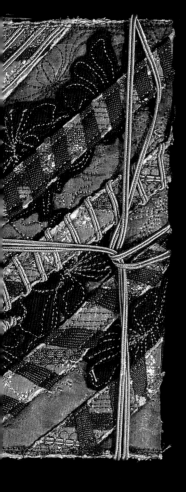

Chapter 7

Gallery

Take time to look through the illustrations in the

Gallery section, which will show you how a number

of embroiderers have used many of the techniques

described in this book.

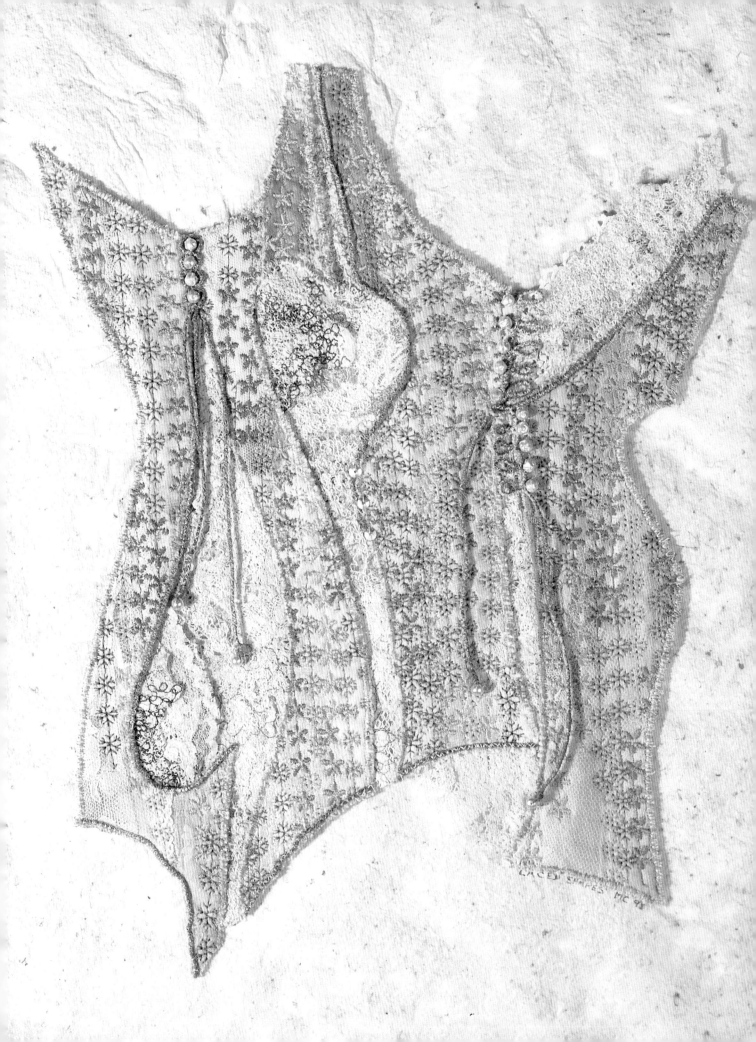

Previous spread: books by Valerie Campbell-Harding using the built-in narrow and larger patterns.

Far left: corset by Margaret Charlton using built-in larger patterns.

Left: mirror by Ruby Lever using a scanned drawing.

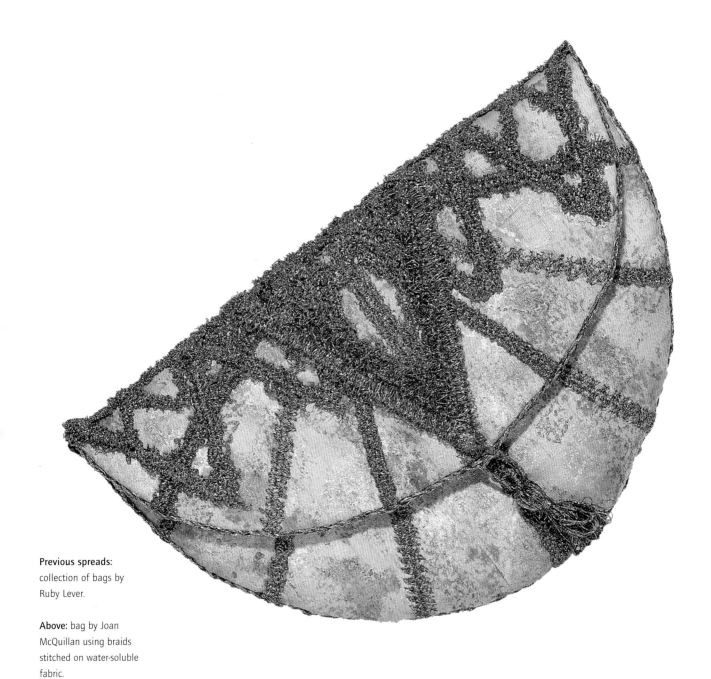

Previous spreads:
collection of bags by
Ruby Lever.

Above: bag by Joan
McQuillan using braids
stitched on water-soluble
fabric.

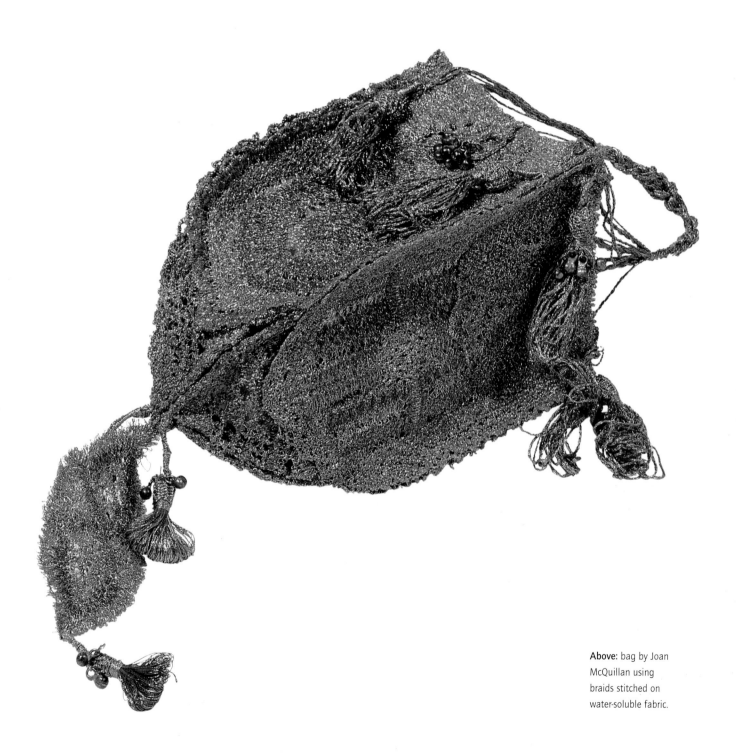

Above: bag by Joan McQuillan using braids stitched on water-soluble fabric.

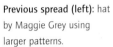

Previous spread (left): hat by Maggie Grey using larger patterns.

Previous spread (right): vessels by Valerie Campbell-Harding using stitched thread braids.

Scroll book by Valerie Campbell-Harding using stitched thread braids.

Tassels by Valerie
Campbell-Harding using a
scanned drawing.

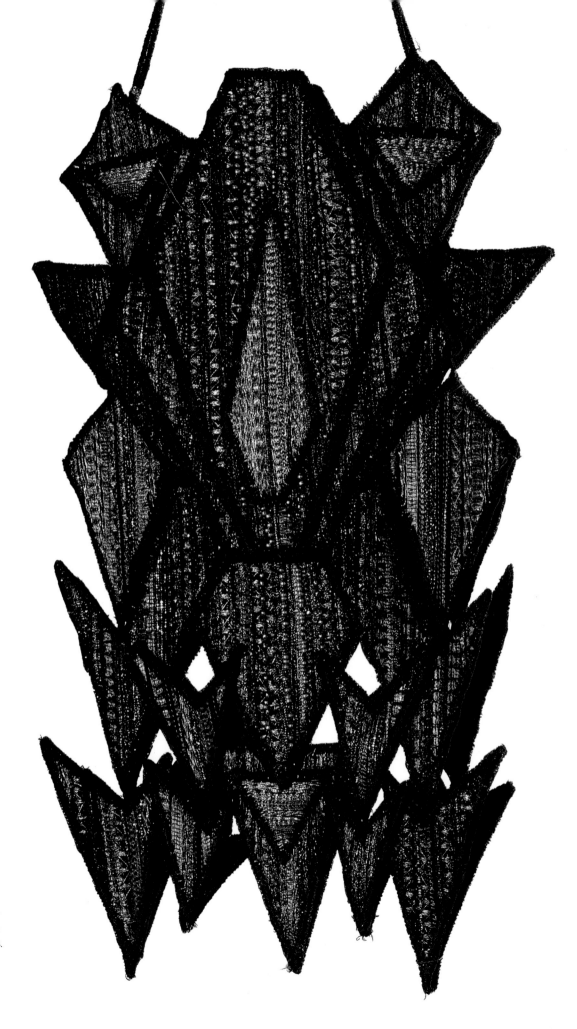

Bag by Valerie Campbell-
Harding showing the use
of different stitch lengths.

FURTHER READING

Art Deco Spot Illustrations and Motifs, William Rowe, Dover Paperbacks 1985

Treasury of Flower Designs, Susan Gaber, Dover Paperbacks 1981

Cover to Cover, Shereen La Plantz, Lark books 1995

Fabric Painting for Embroidery, Valerie Campbell-Harding, Batsford, 1991

Machine Embroidery: Lace and See-through Techniques, Moyra McNeill, Batsford 1985

Machine Embroidery: Stitch Techniques, Valerie Campbell-Harding and Pamela Watts, Batsford 1989

Mbuti Design, Georges Meurant, Thames & Hudson 1995

Shoowa Design, Georges Meurant, Thames & Hudson 1986

The Grammar of Ornament, Owen Jones, Studio Editions 1988

LIST OF SUPPLIERS

SEWING MACHINES

Bernina Sewing Machines
Bogod House
50-52 Great Sutton St.
London EC4 0DJ

Brother Ltd
Shepley Street
Audenshaw
Manchester M34 5JD

Elna Sewing Machines
180-182 Tottenham Court Road
London W1P 9LE

Janome Sewing Machines
Janome Centre
Southside
Bredbury
Stockport
Cheshire SK6 2SP

Pfaff Ltd
Singer UK
Haslemere
Heathrow Estate Parkway
Houndslow TW4 6NX

Singer UK Ltd
91 Coleman Road
Leicester
Leicestershire LE5 4LE

THREADS, FABRICS AND NOTIONS

Borovicks
16 Berwick Street
London W1V 4HP

Shades at Mace & Nairn
89 Crane Street
Salisbury
Wiltshire SP1 2PY

Silken Strands
20 Y Rhos
Bangor LL57 2LT

The Silk Route
32 Wolseley Road
Godalming
Surrey GU7 3EA

TL Threads Ltd
Unit 1
Benneworth Close
Hucknell
Nottingham
Nottinghamshire
NG15 6EL

Hanson's Fabrics
Old Station Yard
Station Road
Sturminster Newton
Dorset DT10 1RD

Nancy's Notions
333 Beichl Avenue
PO Box 683
Beaver's Dam
Wisconsin
WI 53916-5683
USA

Clothilde, Inc
2 Sew Smart Way
Stevens Point
Wisconsin
WI 54481-8031
USA

ART MATERIALS, FABRIC PAINTS

Viv Arthur
Art Van Go
16 Hollybush Lane
Datchworth
Knebworth
Hertfordshire SG3 6RE

George Weil
Reading Arch Road
Redhill
Surrey RH1 1HB

INDEX